Henry Lee

Family prayers

With forms for occasional and private use

Henry Lee

Family prayers

With forms for occasional and private use

ISBN/EAN: 9783337283933

Printed in Europe, USA, Canada, Australia, Japan

Cover: Foto ©Lupo / pixelio.de

More available books at **www.hansebooks.com**

FAMILY PRAYERS;

WITH

FORMS FOR OCCASIONAL AND PRIVATE USE.

BY THE

Rt. Rev. HENRY W. LEE, D. D.,

BISHOP OF THE DIOCESE OF IOWA.

NEW YORK:
E. P DUTTON AND COMPANY,
713 BROADWAY.
1871.

PREFACE.

It is with unfeigned diffidence that the author of this little manual submits the same to the families that call on the name of the Lord. The reasons of its publication are as follows:

It has often occurred to the mind of the author that most of the forms which have been prepared for family devotion are not sufficiently concise. He has, therefore, endeavored to study brevity in those now offered, so that those heads of families who are most busily engaged in the secular concerns of life, may not plead want of time as an excuse for omitting a most solemn and important duty.

In passing over his present Diocesan field, as well as in his former parochial charges, he has often seen the need of some such manual as he has endeavored to prepare. While, therefore, he would particularly dedicate it to the ministers and people of the Diocese whose servant he is for Jesus' sake, and to the parishioners of Christ Church, Springfield, Mass., and of St. Luke's Church, Rochester, N. Y., he would express the hope that they, and all others who may see fit to make use of these simple forms, may so pray to God their heavenly Father, that he may be pleased to accept their bounden duty and service, and grant them, through Jesus Christ, the rich blessings of his grace.

Several prayers are inserted for special occasions, and some have been prepared for young children. It is impossible to make an extravagant estimate of the importance of teaching children the duty of prayer, and of teaching them to pray, by themselves, in language which they can understand. They are sometimes absent from the family circle at the time of family prayer, especially at the evening oblation; and on this account, if for no other reason, they should early learn to pray for themselves. In any case, they should have their own appropriate prayers, and be taught to offer them with reverence and godly fear. It was with such views that the present author prepared, twenty years since, a simple book of prayers for children; and he has the satisfaction of knowing that in not a few instances it has been blessed to the lambs of Christ's flock.

It is to be feared that many persons sadly neglect secret devotion; and doubtless some are thus negligent for want of some guide. A Morning and Evening Prayer have, therefore, been added to meet such cases. The other prayers may properly be used in private by changing the plural to the singular number. It will be well, however, for individuals to substitute their own language where their peculiar wants or feelings are not fully expressed in the forms referred to. And the same may be suggested generally in regard to the family and occasional prayers. Circumstances are constantly transpiring, in both individual and family experience, which require special notice in the closet and at the family altar, and which call for expressions of language which cannot in all cases be fully anticipated in a precomposed and permanent form. This manual is intended chiefly as a helper and general guide; and it is earnestly hoped that it will never quench the spirit of true devotion, either at the domestic fireside, or in the privacy of Christian retirement.

The author is much indebted to other similar works for the materials of which this is composed. Wherever, however, he has availed himself of the language of others, he has generally modified or condensed it, to meet the object which he had in view. It will be seen that the "Forms of Prayer to be used in Families," set forth in the Book of Common Prayer, are inserted entire. The Collects are also added; and it is recommended that they be used, in their season, with the daily prayers.

If this little volume shall, in any instance, be the

means, in the hands of God, of the erection of a family altar; or if it shall afford the least assistance to those who are accustomed to assemble and meet together for family worship, or who call upon Him in secret devotion, the author will thank God, and feel that he has not labored in vain.

DIOCESE OF IOWA, *July*, 1865.

CONTENTS.

FORMS OF PRAYER TO BE USED IN FAMILIES.

	PAGE
Morning Prayer	1
Evening Prayer	5
Sunday Morning	10
Sunday Evening	13
Monday Morning	16
Monday Evening	18
Tuesday Morning	20
Tuesday Evening	22
Wednesday Morning	24
Wednesday Evening	26
Thursday Morning	28
Thursday Evening	31
Friday Morning	33
Friday Evening	35
Saturday Morning	38
Saturday Evening	40
Sunday Morning	43
Sunday Evening	45
Monday Morning	47
Monday Evening	49
Tuesday Morning	51
Tuesday Evening	53
Wednesday Morning	55
Wednesday Evening	58
Thursday Morning	60
Thursday Evening	62
Friday Morning	65
Friday Evening	67
Saturday Morning	69
Saturday Evening	72

OCCASIONAL AND PRIVATE PRAYERS.

	PAGE
Christmas Day	75
The Beginning or Close of a Year	78
Epiphany	80
Ash-Wednesday	83
Good-Friday	85
Easter Day	88
Ascension Day	90
Whit-Sunday	91
Trinity Sunday	94
The Fourth Day of July	95
A Prayer for our Country	98
Thanksgiving Day	99
A Prayer in Time of Public Danger or Troubles	102
A Thanksgiving for Deliverance from Public Calamities	103
Prayer for the Minister	104
A Minister's Prayer for Himself and His People	107
Prayer for an Increase of Laborers in the Lord's Vineyard	109
Prayer for a Blessing on the Diocese	111
Prayer for Unity among all Christian People	112
A Bishop's Prayer for Himself and His Diocese	114
Before Communion	117
Private Prayer before Communion	118
For a Birth-day	122
Prayer after the Birth of a Child	123
Before the Baptism of a Child	124
After the Baptism of a Child	125
After Confirmation	126
For a Sick Member of the Family	126
Thanksgiving for Recovery from Sickness	128
A Sick Person's Prayer	129
For a Sick Child	130
Thanksgiving for the Recovery of a Sick Child	132
Prayer after the Death of a Member of the Family	133
Prayer for an Absent Member of a Family	135
Prayer for a Child Absent at School	135
Thanksgiving for a Safe Return	136
Prayer of Parents for their Children	137
Child's Morning Prayer	139

CONTENTS.

	PAGE
Child's Evening Prayer	140
Morning Prayer for a very Young Child	141
Evening Prayer for a very Young Child	142
Private Prayer. Morning	143
Private Prayer. Evening	146
On Coming into Church	149
On Leaving Church	150
Before or after Meals	151
THE COLLECTS	152–182

FORMS OF PRAYER
TO BE USED IN FAMILIES.

[*From the Book of Common Prayer.*]

Morning Prayer.

¶ The Master or Mistress having called together as many of the Family as can conveniently be present, let one of them, or any other whom they shall think proper, say as follows, all kneeling:

OUR Father, who art in Heaven, Hallowed be thy Name. Thy Kingdom come. Thy Will be done on Earth, as it is in Heaven. Give us this day our daily bread. And forgive us our trespasses, As we forgive those who trespass against us. And lead us not into temptation; But deliver us from evil: For thine is the kingdom, and the power, and the glory, for ever and ever. Amen.

Almighty and everlasting God, in whom we live and move and have our being; we, thy needy creatures, render thee our humble praises, <small>Acknowledgment of God's mercy and preservation, especially through the night past.</small>

for thy preservation of us from the beginning of our lives to this day, and especially for having delivered us from the dangers of the past night. To thy watchful providence we owe it,* (that no disturbance hath come nigh us or our dwelling; but that we are brought in safety to the beginning of this day.) For these thy mercies, we bless and magnify thy glorious Name; humbly beseeching thee to accept this our morning sacrifice of praise and thanksgiving; for his sake who lay down in the grave, and rose again for us, thy Son our Saviour Jesus Christ. *Amen.*

* *When disturbances of any kind befall a Family, instead of this, say, that notwithstanding our dangers, we are brought in safety to the beginning of this day.*

And since it is of thy mercy, O gracious Father, that another day is added to our lives; we here dedicate both our souls and our bodies to thee and thy service, in a sober, righteous, and godly life: in which resolution, do thou, O merciful God, confirm and strengthen us; that, as we grow in age, we may grow in grace, and in the knowledge of our Lord and Saviour Jesus Christ. *Amen.*

Dedication of soul and body to God's service, with a resolution to be growing daily in goodness.

But, O God, who knowest the weakness and corruption of our nature, and the manifold temptations which we daily meet with; we humbly beseech thee to have compassion on our infirmities, and to give us the constant assistance of thy Holy Spirit; that we may be effectually restrained from sin, and excited to our duty. Imprint upon our hearts such a dread of thy judgments, and such a grateful sense of thy goodness to us, as may make us both afraid and ashamed to offend thee. And, above all, keep in our minds a lively remembrance of that great day, in which we must give a strict account of our thoughts, words, and actions; and, according to the works done in the body, be eternally rewarded or punished, by him whom thou hast appointed the Judge of quick and dead, thy Son Jesus Christ our Lord. *Amen.*

<small>Prayer for grace to enable us to perform that resolution.</small>

In particular, we implore thy grace and protection for the ensuing day. Keep us temperate in our meats and drinks, and diligent in our

<small>For grace to guide and keep us the following day, and for God's blessing on the business of the same.</small>

several callings. Grant us patience under any afflictions thou shalt see fit to lay on us, and minds always contented with our present condition. Give us grace to be just and upright in all our dealings; quiet and peaceable; full of compassion; and ready to do good to all men, according to our abilities and opportunities. Direct us in all our ways* (and prosper the works of our hands in the business of our several stations). Defend us from all dangers and adversities; and be graciously pleased to take us, and all things belonging to us, under thy fatherly care and protection. These things, and whatever else thou shalt see necessary and convenient to us, we humbly beg, through the merits and mediation of thy Son Jesus Christ our Lord and Saviour. *Amen.*

* *On Sunday Morning instead of this, say,* and let thy Holy Spirit accompany us to the place of thy public worship, making us serious and attentive, and raising our minds from the thoughts of this world to the consideration of the next, that we may fervently join in the prayers and praises of thy Church, and listen to our duty with honest hearts, in order to practise it.

The grace of our Lord Jesus Christ, and the love of God, and the fellowship of the Holy Ghost, be with us all evermore. *Amen.*

Evening Prayer.

[*From the Book of Common Prayer.*]

OUR Father, who art in Heaven, Hallowed be thy Name. Thy Kingdom come. Thy Will be done on Earth, as it is in Heaven. Give us this day our daily bread. And forgive us our trespasses, As we forgive those who trespass against us. And lead us not into temptation; But deliver us from evil: For thine is the kingdom, and the power, and the glory, for ever and ever. Amen.

Most merciful God, who art of purer eyes than to behold iniquity, and hast promised forgiveness to all those who confess and forsake their sins; we come before thee in an humble sense of our own unworthiness, acknowledging our manifold transgressions of thy righteous laws.* But, O gracious Father, who desirest not the death of a sinner, look upon us, we beseech thee, in mercy, and

Confession of sins, with a prayer for contrition and pardon.

* Here, let him who reads make a short pause, that every one may secretly confess the sins and failings of that day.

forgive us all our transgressions. Make us deeply sensible of the great evil of them; and work in us an hearty contrition; that we may obtain forgiveness at thy hands, who art ever ready to receive humble and penitent sinners; for the sake of thy Son Jesus Christ, our only Saviour and Redeemer. *Amen.*

And lest, through our own frailty, or the temptations which encompass us, we be drawn again into sin, vouchsafe us, we beseech thee, the direction and assistance of thy Holy Spirit. Reform whatever is amiss in the temper and disposition of our souls; that no unclean thoughts, unlawful designs, or inordinate desires, may rest there. Purge our hearts from envy, hatred, and malice; that we may never suffer the sun to go down upon our wrath; but may always go to our rest in peace, charity, and good-will, with a conscience void of offence towards thee and towards men: That so we may be preserved pure and blameless, unto the coming of our Lord and Saviour Jesus Christ. *Amen.*

Prayer for grace to reform and grow better.

And accept, O Lord, our intercessions for all mankind. Let the light of thy Gospel shine upon all nations; and may as many as have received it, live as becomes it. *The Intercession.* Be gracious unto thy Church; and grant that every member of the same, in his vocation and ministry, may serve thee faithfully. Bless all in authority over us; and so rule their hearts and strengthen their hands, that they may punish wickedness and vice, and maintain thy true religion and virtue. Send down thy blessings, temporal and spiritual, upon all our relations, friends, and neighbours. Reward all who have done us good, and pardon all those who have done or wish us evil, and give them repentance and better minds. Be merciful to all who are in any trouble; and do thou, the God of pity, administer to them according to their several necessities, for his sake who went about doing good, thy Son our Saviour Jesus Christ. *Amen.*

To our prayers, O Lord, we join our unfeigned thanks for all thy mercies; for our being, our reason, and all other endowments and faculties of soul and body; for our health, friends, food, and raiment, and all the other comforts and conveniences of life. Above all, we adore thy mercy in sending thy only Son into the world to redeem us from sin and eternal death, and in giving us the knowledge and sense of our duty towards thee. We bless thee for thy patience with us, notwithstanding our many and great provocations; for all the directions, assistances, and comforts of thy Holy Spirit; for thy continual care and watchful providence over us through the whole course of our lives; and particularly for the mercies and benefits of the past day: beseeching thee to continue these thy blessings to us; and to give us grace to show our thankfulness in a sincere obedience to his laws, through whose merits and intercession we received them all, thy Son our Saviour Jesus Christ. *Amen.*

The Thanksgiving.

In particular, we beseech thee to continue thy gracious protection to us this night. Defend us from all dangers and mischiefs, and from the fear of them; that we may enjoy such refreshing sleep as may fit us for the duties of the following day. *Prayer for God's protection through the night following.* Make us ever mindful of the time when we shall lie down in the dust; and grant us grace always to live in such a state, that we may never be afraid to die: so that, living and dying, we may be thine, through the merits and satisfaction of thy Son Christ Jesus, in whose name we offer up these our imperfect prayers. *Amen.*

The grace of our Lord Jesus Christ, and the love of God, and the fellowship of the Holy Ghost, be with us all evermore. *Amen.*

Sunday Morning.

O LORD, our heavenly Father, Almighty and everlasting God, we bless thee for defending us from the perils and dangers of the night past, and for bringing us in safety to the beginning of this holy day. Be with us in all the duties that are now before us, and enable us to worship thee, who art a Spirit, in spirit and in truth. Guide us in our private meditations. May we read and hear thy Word with reverence and godly fear, knowing that it is able to make us wise unto salvation, through faith that is in Christ Jesus.

We confess, O God, that we have greatly polluted many of thy Sabbaths, by doing our own ways, by seeking our own pleasure, and by speaking our own words; and thou mightest justly visit us for our iniquity, by causing them altogether to cease among us.

But thou art a merciful God, full of compassion, long-suffering, and of great pity; sparing us when we deserve punishment, and in the midst of judgment remembering mercy. And we beseech thee, O Lord, still to spare us, and to have mercy upon us. For Jesus' sake, look down upon us, and grant us thy blessing.

May we enter upon the duties of this day as those who know not but that it may be their last, remembering that for all our privileges we must render an account in the day of judgment, and that to whom much is given, of them will much be required.

Prepare us, O God, for the solemnities of thy public worship. Be with all the congregations of thy people, wherever they shall be gathered together in thy name. Bless thy ministering servants, whom thou hast appointed to show unto men the way of salvation. [We would especially commend unto thee thy servant who ministereth unto us. May he faithfully proclaim the truth as it is in Jesus, and declare unto us all the counsel of God. May he be delivered from the fear of man; and, having finished the work which thou hast given him to do, may he at last be received into thy kingdom and glory on high.]

Let the hearts of those rejoice who seek thee faithfully in thy sacred ordinances; and may it please thee to satisfy all with the plenteousness of thy house, and to suffer none to return empty away.

Grant these our humble petitions, for thy mercy's sake in Jesus Christ, our only Lord and Saviour. *Amen.*

Our Father, who art in Heaven, Hallowed be thy Name. Thy Kingdom come. Thy Will be done on Earth, as it is in Heaven. Give us this day our daily bread. And forgive us our trespasses, As we forgive those who trespass against us. And lead us not into temptation; But deliver us from evil: For thine is the kingdom, and the power, and the glory, for ever and ever. Amen.

The grace of our Lord Jesus Christ, and the love of God, and the fellowship of the Holy Ghost, be with us all evermore. *Amen.*

Sunday Evening.

O ALMIGHTY Lord and everlasting God, hear our prayer which we make before thee at the close of this sacred day, and accept our thanks for all thy mercies. We bless thee for the means of grace which we have enjoyed, and for the hope of glory which has been set before us in the Gospel of thy dear Son.

Give us, we beseech thee, that due sense of all thy mercies, that our hearts may be unfeignedly thankful, and that our lives may be devoted to thy service. May it be our constant desire and endeavor to render unto thee according to thy benefits, walking before thee in holiness and righteousness all our days.

Bless thy Word, O Lord, wherever it has this day been spoken, and send it where it is not heard. May the time soon come when at the name of Jesus every knee shall bow, and every tongue shall confess that he is Lord, to the glory of God the Father.

May Christ be made unto each and all of us wisdom, and righteousness, and sanctification, and redemption; and may all our glorying be in him. O God, forbid that we should glory, save in the cross of our Lord Jesus Christ, by whom the world is crucified unto us, and we unto the world. May we ever remember that his is the only name given under heaven among men whereby we can be saved, and may we trust in him as our all in all.

Extend thy mercy, O Lord, to thy Church universal, and especially to that branch of it with which we are connected. May all who are called Christians be led into the way of truth, and walk worthy of their high and holy vocation. Bless the congregation with which we are accustomed to worship, as well as thy servant to whose charge it is committed. Graft in all our hearts a love of the truth; increase in us true religion; nourish us with all goodness; and, of thy great mercy, keep us in the same, so that in the end we may obtain everlasting life.

Be with us, O Lord, during the darkness of this night, and finally save us in thy kingdom, through Jesus Christ, our strength and our Redeemer. *Amen.*

Our Father, who art in Heaven, Hallowed be thy Name Thy Kingdom come. Thy Will be done on Earth, as it is in Heaven. Give us this day our daily bread. And forgive us our trespasses, As we forgive those who trespass against us. And lead us not into temptation; But deliver us from evil: For thine is the kingdom, and the power, and the glory, for ever and ever. Amen.

The grace of our Lord Jesus Christ, and the love of God, and the fellowship of the Holy Ghost, be with us all· evermore. *Amen.*

Monday Morning.

O LORD, our heavenly Father, help us to come before thee under a deep sense of our unworthiness, and in humble reliance on thy goodness and compassion.

By thy good providence we have been preserved through the past night, and we would begin the day with a renewed dedication of ourselves to thy service. Give us grace to be diligent and faithful in all the duties upon which we are now to enter, and may we remember that thine eye is continually upon us, that thou knowest the thoughts of our hearts, and searchest out all our ways. Preserve us from danger and from sin; and grant that all our doings, being ordered by thy governance, may be righteous in thy sight.

Be with us, O Lord, in all the journey of life. Cause us to be penitent, and submissive to thy will; and give us such knowledge and sense of thy goodness and of our duty, that while we live we may live to thee. May we be a united and happy family here on the earth, and at last be admitted, as members of thy redeemed family, to the joys of thy heavenly kingdom.

Be pleased, O Lord, to bestow on others the blessings we have implored for ourselves. Be merciful to all our relatives and friends, and make them partakers of thy grace here, and of thy glory hereafter.

And thus, when we have passed the waves of this troublesome world, may we all come to the land of everlasting life, through Jesus Christ our Saviour. *Amen.*

Our Father, who art in Heaven, &c.

The grace of our Lord Jesus Christ, &c.

Monday Evening.

O Almighty and most merciful God, we approach the throne of thy grace to praise thee for thy goodness through the past day, and to implore thy continued protection this night.

We thank thee that thou hast this day kept us from danger and from death; and wilt thou guard us this night from the pestilence that walketh in darkness, and bring us in safety to the light of another day.

Give us hearts, O Lord, to be thankful for thy manifold goodness to us and to all men; and make us deeply penitent for all our sins. We have erred and strayed from thy righteous ways, and offended against thy holy laws. But wilt thou hide thy face from our sins, and blot out all our iniquities; and may we ever hereafter serve and please thee in newness of life.

Thou seest that we have no power of ourselves to help ourselves. Take us, therefore, we beseech thee, under the protection of thy good providence. Keep us, both outwardly in our bodies, and inwardly in our souls, that we may be defended from all adversities which may happen to the body, and from all evil thoughts which may assault and hurt the soul.

Extend thy mercy, O Lord, to all for whom we should pray. Send down thy blessings, temporal and spiritual, upon our relatives, friends, and neighbors. Be merciful to all who are in any trouble, and visit and relieve them according to their several necessities, giving them patience under their sufferings, and a happy issue out of all their afflictions. Pour out thy Spirit upon all mankind, and may the time soon come when the whole earth shall be filled with thy glory; through Jesus Christ, our strength and our Redeemer. *Amen.*

Our Father, who art in Heaven, &c.

The grace of our Lord Jesus Christ, &c.

Tuesday Morning.

ALMIGHTY and ever-blessed God, we would prostrate ourselves before thy mercy-seat this morning, beseeching thee to assist us in these our supplications and prayers, and to dispose our ways towards the attainment of everlasting salvation.

Through thy mercy we have been preserved through the silent watches of the night, while many of our fellow-creatures have slept the sleep of death, and shall awake no more till the resurrection at the last day. Lord, what are we, that thou shouldst be so mindful of us, and so gracious unto us, in saving our life from destruction, and crowning us with loving-kindness and tender mercies! We confess that thou art the Lord by whom alone we have escaped death, and our praise shall be always of thee.

With the light of the morning lift thou upon us the light of thy countenance, and guide and protect us through the day. Not knowing what a day may bring forth, may we put our whole trust and confidence in thy mercy, and live in constant readiness for the eternal world. May Christ dwell in our hearts by faith, and may he be formed in us, the hope of glory. May we cling to his cross, and follow the blessed steps of his most holy life.

And grant, O Lord, that as we are baptized into the death of thy blessed Son our Saviour Jesus Christ, so, by continual mortifying our corrupt affections, we may be buried with him; and that through the grave and gate of death we may pass to our joyful resurrection, for his merits, who died and was buried, and rose again for us, thy Son Jesus Christ our Lord. *Amen.*

Our Father, who art in Heaven, &c.

The grace of our Lord Jesus Christ, &c.

Tuesday Evening.

ALMIGHTY Father, who of thy tender love hast given thine only Son, our Saviour Jesus Christ, to suffer death upon the cross for our redemption, that he might deliver us from this present evil world, and save us forever, mercifully look down upon us this night, pardon our sins, and bless us for his sake.

In thy good providence we are brought to the close of another day; and we now commend ourselves to thy care and keeping through the darkness of the night. Make us mindful of the time when we shall lie down in the dust, and grant us grace always to live in such a state that we may never be afraid to die. While we live, may Christ be our life; and when we die, may death be our gain.

Save us, O God, we beseech thee, by the power of the Holy Ghost, from the dominion of sin. Incline our hearts unto thy testimonies, and not to covetousness. May we never be drawn aside from the narrow way of life, to seek after deceitful and uncertain riches. Preserve us from the temptations and snares, and the many foolish and hurtful lusts, which drown men in destruction and perdition. May we use this world as not abusing it; and by patient continuance in well-doing, seek for glory, honor, and immortality in the world to come.

Bless us, O Lord, as a family and household, and visit us with thy love and favor. [May our children be under thy special care and guidance. May they be dutiful and obedient, and remember thee, their Creator, in the days of their childhood and youth. Preserve them from the wickedness that is in the world, and help us to bring them up in the nurture and admonition of the Lord.] Bless our kindred, friends, and brethren; and finally save us all in thy kingdom, through the merits and satisfaction of Jesus Christ, our only Saviour and Redeemer. *Amen.*

Our Father, who art in Heaven, &c.

The grace of our Lord Jesus Christ, &c.

Wednesday Morning.

O LORD our God, in knowledge of whom standeth our eternal life, grant us grace to come before thee at this time under a deep sense of our unworthiness, and in humble reliance on thy goodness and compassion.

We confess, O God, our sinfulness; and we beseech thee, for Christ's sake, to show thy mercy upon us, and to grant us thy salvation. Create and make in us new and contrite hearts, that we, worthily lamenting our sins, and acknowledging our wretchedness, may obtain of thee, the God of all mercy, perfect remission and forgiveness; and may we ever hereafter live to the honor and glory of thy holy name.

Enable us, O God, from day to day, to call to remembrance the solemn vows and promises of our baptism; and may we, by thy grace, avoid those things that are contrary to our profession, and follow all such things as are agreeable to the same, ever looking unto Jesus as the author and finisher of our faith, and putting our trust in him as all our salvation and all our desire. May we fight manfully under his banner, against sin, the world, and the devil; and continue his faithful soldiers and servants unto our life's end. May we be united to him by a living faith; and may thy Spirit bear witness with our spirit that we are thy children, and joint-heirs with Christ to the glories of thy heavenly kingdom.

And now, O Lord, our heavenly Father, who hast safely brought us to the beginning of this day, defend us in the same with thy mighty power; and grant that this day we fall into no sin, neither run into any kind of danger; but that all our doings, being ordered by thy governance, may be righteous in thy sight, through Jesus Christ our Lord. *Amen.*

Our Father who art in Heaven, &c.

The grace of our Lord Jesus Christ, &c.

Wednesday Evening.

ALMIGHTY God, the Father of our Lord Jesus Christ, who desirest not the death of a sinner, but rather that he may turn from his wickedness and live; we beseech thee to grant us true repentance and thy Holy Spirit, that those things may please thee which we do at this present; and that the rest of our life hereafter may be pure and holy; so that at the last we may come to thy eternal joy.

Have mercy upon us, O God, after thy great goodness; according to the multitude of thy tender mercies, do away our offences. Wash us thoroughly from our wickedness, and cleanse us from our sin : for we acknowledge our faults, and our sin is ever before us. Create in us a clean heart, O God, and renew a right spirit within us. Cast us not away from thy presence, and take not thy Holy Spirit from us. O give us the comfort of thy help again, and uphold us with thy free Spirit. Open thou our lips, and our mouth shall show forth thy praise. For thy Son our Lord Jesus Christ's sake, forgive us all that is past, and enable us henceforth to live as those who have been bought with a price, and whose bounden duty it is to glorify thee in our bodies and in our spirits, which are thine.

Accept our thanks, O Lord, for the mercies and benefits of the past day, and for all thy goodness and loving-kindness to us and to all men. It is in thee that we live, and move, and have our being; and from thy bountiful hand we receive every blessing that we enjoy. O give us that due sense of all thy mercies, that our hearts may be unfeignedly thankful, and that we may show forth thy praise by an humble and obedient walking before thee all our days.

Lighten our darkness, we beseech thee, O Lord; and by thy great mercy defend us from all perils and dangers of this night; for the love of thy only Son, our Saviour Jesus Christ. *Amen.*

Our Father, who art in Heaven, &c.

The grace of our Lord Jesus Christ, &c.

Thursday Morning.

O ETERNAL God, who art the Father of all the families of the earth, we bow before thee to thank thee for the mercies of the past night, and to acknowledge that it is by thy power and goodness that we are preserved from day to day. Protect us, we beseech thee, this day from all evil. Be with us in all the duties which are before us, and enable us to do everything in thy fear, and to thy glory. May we undertake nothing which is contrary to thy will, and engage in no pursuit upon which we cannot implore and expect thy blessing.

O Lord, may we remember this day and every day that thine eye is continually upon us, and that all our thoughts and words and actions are known unto thee. Grant us, we pray thee, the assistance of thy Holy Spirit, that we may be effectually restrained from sin and excited to our duty. May we keep in our minds a lively remembrance of that great day when every thought and word and deed will be judged in righteousness. Prepare us, O God, for our final account. As we approach nearer and nearer the eternal world, may we be more diligent and watchful and faithful. As we grow in age, may we grow in grace, and in the knowledge of our Lord and Saviour Jesus Christ. May we lay aside every weight, and the sins that most easily beset us, and run with patience and zeal the race that is set before us. May we ever look unto Jesus as our only hope, and endeavor in all things to follow the blessed steps of his most holy life.

Pardon all our sins, O Lord, and help us to walk before thee in holiness and righteousness all our days; and when we shall have served thee in our generation, and finished the work which thou has given us to do, may we enter into that rest which remaineth to thy faithful people, and which thou hast promised to all those who unfeignedly love thee.

We present these our imperfect prayers in the name of Jesus Christ, our most blessed Lord and Saviour. *Amen.*

Our Father, who art in Heaven, Hallowed be thy Name. Thy Kingdom come. Thy Will be done on Earth, as it is in Heaven. Give us this day our daily bread. And forgive us our trespasses, As we forgive those who trespass against us. And lead us not into temptation; But deliver us from evil: For thine is the kingdom, and the power, and the glory, for ever and ever. Amen.

The grace of our Lord Jesus Christ, and the love of God, and the fellowship of the Holy Ghost, be with us all evermore. *Amen.*

Thursday Evening.

O LORD our God, we come into thy presence to praise thee for thy mercies to us this day, and to implore thy gracious protection through the night. By thy good providence our lives have been preserved, while many of our fellow-creatures have this day been called into the eternal world. Be with us in the hours of darkness, and permit us to see the light of another day. Pardon, O Lord, all the sins of this day, and of our past lives; and may we go to our rest at peace with thee, and in perfect charity with the world.

Be pleased, O Lord, to hear our prayers for all mankind. Let the light of thy Gospel shine upon all nations; and may as many as have received it live as becomes it. Have mercy upon the land in which we dwell. Bless all who are in authority, that they may truly and impartially administer justice, to the punishment of wickedness and vice, and to the maintenance of thy true religion and virtue. Give grace, O heavenly Father, to all Bishops and other ministers, that they may, both by their life and doctrine, set forth thy true and lively Word, and rightly and duly administer thy holy sacraments. And to all thy people give thy heavenly grace; and especially to the congregation with which we are connected. Bless us with all spiritual blessings in Christ Jesus. Bless him who is placed over us as our pastor and teacher in holy things. Make him a faithful shepherd of thy flock, and at last give him a crown of life in thy kingdom and glory.

Send down thy blessings, temporal and spiritual, upon all our relatives, friends, and neighbors. Be merciful to all who are in any trouble, and do thou, the God of pity, administer to them according to their several necessities, giving them patience under their sufferings, and a happy issue out of all their afflictions.

Hear us, O Lord, in these our prayers, in the name and for the sake of Jesus Christ, our Saviour and Redeemer. *Amen.*

Our Father, who art in Heaven, &c.

The grace of our Lord Jesus Christ, &c.

Friday Morning.

ALMIGHTY and most merciful Father, we would this morning humble ourselves before thee as miserable offenders, beseeching thee to be gracious unto us, and to lift upon us the light of thy countenance. We have erred and strayed from thy ways like lost sheep, and followed too much the devices and desires of our own hearts. Have mercy upon us, O Lord, for Christ's sake, and grant us perfect remission and forgiveness. May Christ dwell in each of our hearts by faith, that we, being rooted and grounded in love, may be able to comprehend, with all saints, what is the length, and breadth, and height, and depth, and may know the love of Christ, which passeth knowledge, that we may be filled with all the fulness of God. O may we be crucified unto the world, and the world unto us. May the love of Christ constrain us, and may his grace be sufficient for us in every time of need.

Be with us, O Lord, during this day, and grant us thy blessing. Keep us from danger and from sin. Direct us in all our doings with thy most gracious favor, and further us with thy continual help, that in all our works, begun, continued, and ended in thee, we may glorify thy holy name. Bless us as a family and household, and make us at last members of thy family in heaven. [Bless our children, and give us grace to train them up in thy fear. Preserve them from the wickedness that is in the world, and finally save them in thy kingdom.] Bless all our friends and relatives, wherever, in thy providence, they may be. Make them obedient and submissive to thy will here, that they may become partakers of thy glory hereafter. Bless thy Church universal, and may all who are called Christians walk in the ways of truth and peace, and finally be numbered with thy saints in thy heavenly kingdom. Pour out thy Spirit upon all mankind, and may the whole earth be speedily filled with the knowledge of the Lord, as the waters cover the sea.

We ask every blessing in the name of Jesus Christ, our only Saviour and Redeemer. *Amen.*

Our Father, who art in Heaven, &c.

The grace of our Lord Jesus Christ, &c.

Friday Evening.

LET thy merciful ears, O Lord, be open to the prayers of thy humble servants; and that we may obtain our petitions, make us to ask such things as shall please thee, through Jesus Christ our Lord.

Thou hast graciously assured us that thou hast no pleasure in the death of a sinner, but rather that he be converted and live. Help us, therefore, to confess our iniquity with that godly sorrow which worketh repentance unto salvation, not to be repented of; and to approach thee with the sacrifice of a broken and contrite heart, which thou, O God, wilt not despise. Look down upon us through the Son of thy love, in whom thou canst be just, and yet the justifier of all who truly believe in him. For his sake pardon our manifold sins, and grant us thy salvation.

Accept our thanks, O Lord, for the mercies and benefits of the past day; and command thy blessing to rest upon us through the night season. Hide us under the shadow of thy almighty wings till the perils and dangers of darkness shall have passed away. O make us mindful of the time when we shall lie down in the dust, and sleep the sleep of death; and grant us grace always to live in such a state that we may never be afraid nor unprepared to die. May it be Christ for us to live, and to die be our unspeakable and everlasting gain.

May it please thee, O Lord, to have mercy upon all men. Heal the distractions of thy Church, and pour down upon it the spirit of unity and godly love. Assemble the outcasts of Israel, and gather together the dispersed of Judah. Relieve the oppressed; provide for the poor and needy; preserve all sick persons and young children; comfort all that mourn; show thy pity upon the heathen; and fill the earth with thy glory.

Hear us, O Lord, in these our prayers; and when thou hearest, answer and forgive, in the name and through the merits of Jesus Christ, our most blessed Lord and Saviour. *Amen.*

Our Father, who art in Heaven, &c.

The grace of our Lord Jesus Christ, &c.

Saturday Morning.

ALMIGHTY and everlasting God, we bow before thee to thank thee for all thy goodness and loving-kindness, and especially for thy merciful care and protection during the past night. Help us to begin the day with the solemn dedication of ourselves to thy service; and may we go to the duties of our several stations with an earnest desire to do everything in thy fear, and with a view to thy glory.

O Lord, grant unto us thy Holy Spirit. May it dwell within us as a spirit of purity and holiness, a spirit of truth and of wisdom, of peace also, and love, and of holy joy and consolation. May we pass this day in a thankful remembrance of thy mercies, and in the diligent performance of thy commandments. May we faithfully fulfil the duties of the day; and may we lie down at night, praising thee again for all thy goodness, and committing ourselves with holy confidence to thy mercy.

We pray, that, as our days pass away, we may improve the time that is allotted to us, and give all diligence to make our calling and our election sure. May we have our conversation in heaven, moderating our affections towards the things of this world, and living the life which we live here below by faith in the Son of God. Give us a deep sense of our sinfulness, and help us to lay hold on the hope set before us in the Gospel. May we be steadfast and unmovable, always abounding in the work of the Lord, ever looking unto Jesus as the author and finisher of our faith, and rejoicing in him as our all in all.

Be with us, O Lord, throughout the journey of life. Be with us in all time of our tribulation, and in all time of our prosperity, in the hour of death, and in the day of judgment. And at last, when we shall have finished our course here on the earth, and given an account of ourselves to thee, may we be forever with thee in thy kingdom and glory; through him who loved us and gave himself for us, thy Son Jesus Christ our Saviour. *Amen.*

Our Father, who art in Heaven, &c.

The grace of our Lord Jesus Christ, &c.

Saturday Evening.

O LORD our heavenly Father, by whose almighty power we have been preserved this day, accept our humble and hearty thanks for this and for every manifestation of thy providential goodness. It is a good thing to give thanks unto thee, O Lord, and to sing praises unto thy name, O Most Highest; to tell of thy loving-kindness early in the morning, and of thy truth in the night season.

Pardon, O Lord, the sins of the past day and week, and give us grace hereafter to live more to the honor and glory of thy name. Watch over us this night, and prepare us for the duties and solemnities of the coming day. May we remember that our days are swiftly passing away, and that the night will soon come when no man can work. May we be diligent and active in our Christian calling, and strive to enter into that rest which remaineth to thy faithful people.

We pray for thy blessing upon thy Church, and upon all mankind. May grace, mercy, and peace be upon all that love our Lord Jesus Christ in sincerity, and may the time be hastened on when all the kingdoms of this world shall become the kingdoms of thy dear Son.

Give grace, O heavenly Father, to the ministers and stewards of thy mysteries, and especially to him who is placed over us in thy Name. Wilt thou so replenish them with the truth of thy doctrine, and endue them with innocency of life, that they may faithfully serve before thee, to the glory of thy great name, and the benefit of thy holy Church.

Have mercy upon the poor, the sick, and the afflicted. Make them submissive to thy will, and grant them the consolations of thy heavenly grace. Bless all our friends, relatives, and brethren. May they have that godliness which has the promise of the life that now is, and of that which is to come.

Accept, O Lord, this our evening sacrifice of prayer and thanksgiving, in the name and for the sake of Jesus Christ, our most blessed Redeemer. *Amen.*

Our Father, who art in Heaven, Hallowed be thy Name. Thy Kingdom come. Thy Will be done on Earth, as it is in Heaven. Give us this day our daily bread. And forgive us our trespasses, As we forgive those who trespass against us. And lead us not into temptation ; But deliver us from evil: For thine is the kingdom, and the power, and the glory, for ever and ever. Amen.

The grace of our Lord Jesus Christ, and the love of God, and the fellowship of the Holy Ghost, be with us all evermore. *Amen.*

Sunday Morning.

ALMIGHTY God, Father of our Lord Jesus Christ, Maker of all things, Judge of all men, we adore thee for thy great goodness in providing for our temporal necessities, and more especially we bless thee for the rich provision which thou hast made for the welfare of our immortal souls.

We thank thee that we are brought in safety to the beginning of this holy day; and we pray thee to direct and bless us in all its duties and privileges, and to help us to worship thee in the beauty of holiness. May we hallow thy Sabbaths, and reverence thy sanctuary. Let thy quickening Spirit make us serious, devout, and attentive in every part of thy sacred service.

May thy blessing everywhere accompany the preaching of thy holy Gospel. Pour down the abundance of thy grace on the ministers of Christ, and on the people of their charge. May careless sinners be awakened to a sense of their danger. May unbelievers be convinced. May the young be guided in the right way; and may weak and afflicted souls be comforted. May the borders of thine universal Church be enlarged, and may its members be built up in faith, and hope, and love.

Pardon, O Lord, our manifold sins, and remember them no more against us; and may we ever hereafter serve and please thee in newness of life, to the honor and praise of thy holy name.

Bless all our dear relatives and friends. May they be partakers of thy grace in this life, and in the world to come obtain that life which is everlasting.

Bless our rulers and our country. Visit us not in judgment for our many sins; but give unto us true repentance, and make us that happy people whose God is the Lord.

Have mercy upon a world lying in wickedness, and hasten on the time when all the nations shall rejoice in thy salvation.

We offer these our imperfect prayers in the name and through the merits of Jesus Christ, our only Mediator and Redeemer *Amen.*

Our Father, who art in Heaven, &c.

The grace of our Lord Jesus Christ, &c.

Sunday Evening.

BLESSED be thy name, O Lord, for all the mercies and benefits of the past day. We thank thee for the means of grace, and for the hope of glory. Above all, we adore thee for the gift of thy dear Son our Saviour Jesus Christ, who is our Advocate with thee, and the Lord our Righteousness. May we be complete in him, and may we glory only in his cross.

Sanctify to us the solemn services of this day; and may we show forth in our lives the holy teachings of thy word, and the sacred influence of thy hallowed day of rest.

We implore thy mercy upon all those nations and people that are yet sitting in darkness and the shadow of death. May thy especial blessing rest on all who are laboring to extend to them the knowledge of a crucified Redeemer. Open the hearts of the heathen to receive thy Gospel in the love of it. May the wilderness and the solitary place be made glad, and the desert rejoice and blossom as the rose. May thine ancient people Israel see in Jesus the true Messiah, and may every tongue soon confess that he is Lord, to the glory of God the Father.

Defend us, O God, from all perils and dangers of this night, and take us and all who are near and dear to us under thy fatherly care and protection; through Jesus Christ, our most blessed Lord and Saviour. *Amen.*

Our Father, who art in Heaven, &c.

The grace of our Lord Jesus Christ, &c.

Monday Morning.

O LORD, our God, by whose gracious Providence all our affairs are daily ordered and directed; incline thine ear to us, thy dependent creatures, to whom thou hast vouchsafed the light of another day.

We thank thee for the preservation of our lives, and for all the blessings that we enjoy; and we humbly ask for the continuance of thy goodness. Defend us this day from danger and from sin, and give us such things as are needful for our present comfort, and for our eternal good. Keep us ever mindful of our dependence upon thee, and quicken us in the pursuit of things eternal. Dispose us rightly to discharge the duties of this day. Watch over our paths, and direct all our steps in the way of thy commandments. May we be honest and upright in all our dealings; diligent in our calling; and mindful of thy continual presence. May we realize that we know not what a day may bring forth, and that in the midst of life we are in death; and by thy grace may we be in constant readiness for the time of our departure, and for the world to come.

Bless those near and dear to us who are absent from us, and grant unto them the gifts of thy grace, and the joys of thy salvation.

Bless thy universal Church, and may all those who do confess thy holy Name agree in the truth of thy holy Word, and live in unity and godly love. Give grace to all Bishops and other Ministers; that they may, both by their life and doctrine, set forth thy true and lively Word, and rightly and duly administer thy holy sacraments. And do thou, O Lord of the harvest, increase the number of laborers in thy harvest, till thy Gospel shall be preached to every creature, and all shall know thee from the least even unto the greatest.

Pardon, O Lord, the coldness and imperfection of our prayers, and forgive all our sins; through the merits and satisfaction of our blessed Saviour and Redeemer, Jesus Christ, to whom, with thee and the Holy Ghost, be all honor and glory, world without end. *Amen.*

Our Father, who art in Heaven, &c.

The grace of our Lord Jesus Christ, &c.

Monday Evening.

O Thou in whom we live, and move, and have our being; we reverence thy glorious majesty, and adore thine infinite mercy. We humble ourselves before thee as miserable offenders, beseeching thee to spare us, though we deserve punishment, and to grant us perfect remission and forgiveness. We have nothing to plead but thy promises. O be merciful unto us, for the glory of thy Name. Restore our souls, for we have sinned against thee. May we be justified by faith, and have peace with thee, O God, through Jesus Christ.

We thank thee, O Lord, for thy care over us this day; and we now pray thee to keep us in safety through this night. Make us mindful of death and eternity; and may we never forget that we must soon lie down, to rise no more till the last great day. O when we die, may we fall asleep in Jesus, who is the life of them that believe, and the resurrection of the dead: may we go down to the grave full of the blessed hope of everlasting life.

Bless, we beseech thee, all whom we should remember before thee; and do for us, for our dear children, relatives, and friends, for thy Church, for our rulers and our country, and for all mankind, abundantly above all that we are able to ask or think; for Jesus Christ's sake: in whose name and words we further pray, saying,

Our Father, who art in Heaven, &c.

The grace of our Lord Jesus Christ, &c.

Tuesday Morning.

O LORD our God, we adore thy Name, which is excellent in all the earth, and whose glory is above the heavens. We bless thee for the rest and preservation of the night past. O cause us to hear thy loving kindness in the morning, for in thee do we trust. Make us to know the way wherein we should go, for which we would continue daily to lift up our soul unto thee. Cast us not away from thy presence, nor take thy Holy Spirit from us; but direct our hearts into thy love, and our feet into the way of thy testimonies. May we be ever found in the way of duty, fearing God and working righteousness; walking in the steps of thy blessed Son; making it evident to all that we are influenced by his Spirit, guided by his example, and pressing forward to his kingdom. Day by day would we magnify thee, O Lord, and worship thy Name for ever and ever.

We beseech thee to take us this day under thy holy care and keeping. Direct us in all our doings with thy most gracious favor, and further us with thy continual help. May we honor thee in our lives, and in all our works and ways glorify thy holy Name. May we remember that our days are swiftly passing away, and may we live in constant preparation for the hour of death and the day of judgment.

Bless us as a family, and make us at last members of thy family in heaven. Bless our absent friends, and make them thy friends, and partakers of thy heavenly kingdom. Have pity upon the sick and sorrowful, and administer to them according to their several necessities. Bring all mankind to a knowledge of the truth, and make all nations to rejoice in thy salvation, through Jesus Christ, thine only Son our Lord and Saviour. *Amen.*

Our Father, who art in Heaven, &c.

The grace of our Lord Jesus Christ, &c.

Tuesday Evening.

O MOST merciful God and heavenly Father, Giver of all spiritual grace, the Author of everlasting life ; we, thy sinful creatures, desire to confess before thee our unworthiness, and to laud and magnify thy holy Name. We are miserable offenders, and are not worthy of the least of thy mercies; but thou, O Lord, art full of compassion, long-suffering, and of great goodness. Have mercy upon us, most merciful Father, and pardon all our transgressions. Make us deeply sensible of the great evil of them, and work in us an hearty contrition, that we may obtain forgiveness at thy hands, who art ever ready to receive humble and penitent sinners, for the sake of thy dear Son. And may we henceforth live according to thy will, and walk before thee in holiness and righteousness all our days.

Accept our thanks, O Lord, for the mercies of the past day, and continue thy gracious protection to us this night. May we lie down in peace, and take our rest, knowing that it is thou, Lord, only that makest us to dwell in safety.

Be gracious unto thy Church, and grant that every member of the same, in his vocation and ministry, may serve thee faithfully. Endue the ministers of thy Gospel with thy heavenly grace. Increase their number, and encourage their hearts. Bless the congregation with which we are connected, and our pastor and teacher in the Lord. Bless our Bishop and our Diocese. May we all be built up a holy temple acceptable to thee, and be made a habitation of God through the Spirit.

Extend the light of thy truth throughout the world. Give to all nations unity, peace, and concord. Relieve the oppressed; succor the destitute and the afflicted; be the Father of the fatherless, and the God of the widow; bind up the broken-hearted, and save such as be of a contrite spirit; giving them everlasting consolation and good hope, through thy grace and mercy in Christ Jesus.

We ask for all in the Name and for the sake of the same, thy Son, our Saviour Jesus Christ. *Amen.*

Our Father, who art in Heaven, &c.

The grace of our Lord Jesus Christ, &c.

Wednesday Morning.

O LORD our heavenly Father, whose power is infinite, and whose mercy is everlasting; we, thy sinful and dependent creatures, most humbly thank thee for thy providential care of us during the past night, and we beseech thee to watch over us and protect us throughout this day. Save us from all things that can harm the body, and especially from whatsoever can assault and hurt the soul. May we this day be set forward in our Christian course; and as we approach nearer and nearer to the eternal world, may we give increased diligence to prepare to meet thee, our God. As we grow in age, may we grow in grace and in the knowledge of our Lord and Saviour Jesus Christ. May we daily increase in thy Holy Spirit more and more, until we come unto thy everlasting kingdom.

Deliver us, O Lord, from the guilt and power of sin. May we set our affection on things above, and not on things on the earth. May we become dead unto sin, and may our life be hid with Christ in God; so that when Christ, who is our life, shall appear, we may also appear with him in glory. May we, by thy grace, mortify our members which are on the earth, crucifying the flesh with its affections and lusts, and finally beating down Satan under our feet.

To thy grace and love, O heavenly Father, we now commend ourselves and all our relatives, friends, and brethren. Keep, we beseech thee, thy Church with thy perpetual mercy. Heal its divisions, and drive from it all erroneous and strange doctrines contrary to thy Word. Bless the land in which we dwell. Save us from deserved punishment, and make us to be a people fearing thee and working righteousness.

Finally, we pray thee, O thou God of all the families of the earth, to hasten the time when thy saving health shall be known among all nations, and when there shall be none to hurt or destroy in all thy holy mountain; through Jesus Christ our Saviour. *Amen.*

Our Father, who art in Heaven, Hallowed be thy Name. Thy Kingdom come. Thy Will be done on Earth, as it is in Heaven. Give us this day our daily bread. And forgive us our trespasses, As we forgive those who trespass against us. And lead us not into temptation; But deliver us from evil: For thine is the kingdom, and the power, and the glory, for ever and ever. Amen.

The grace of our Lord Jesus Christ, and the love of God, and the fellowship of the Holy Ghost, be with us all evermore. *Amen.*

Wednesday Evening.

ALMIGHTY GOD, Father of all mercies, accept our united and hearty thanks for all the blessings thou hast bestowed upon us, and especially for those we have received during the past day. May thy goodness lead us to repentance; and may we show forth thy praise, not only with our lips, but in our lives, by giving up ourselves to thy service, and by walking before thee in holiness and righteousness all our days. Enable us henceforth to be more watchful against temptation, and more faithful and diligent in doing our duty in that state of life to which thou hast called us. May we renewedly consecrate ourselves to thee, and devote all our powers and faculties to the promotion of thy glory. May all our wishes and desires centre in what thou hast commanded, and may we press toward the mark for the prize of the high calling of God, in Christ Jesus. Purify our hearts from all sinful affections, and keep us ever steadfast in thy fear and love. Grant us such temporal blessings as thy wisdom shall see expedient for us; and may thy good Providence, which has guarded us through the day, be our protection through the night.

We beseech thee, also, to protect our relatives and friends, and to forgive our enemies. Relieve the wants of all thy creatures. Bless our civil rulers, and guide their steps in the way of thy commandments. May all the people of this land obey thy will, and observe thy laws. Pour down thy Holy Spirit on all the bishops and other pastors of thy Church; and to all thy people give thy heavenly grace, that they may run with patience the race that is set before them, and finally receive the crown of everlasting life; through our Lord and Saviour Jesus Christ. *Amen.*

Our Father, who art in Heaven, &c.

The grace of our Lord Jesus Christ, &c.

Thursday Morning.

O ALMIGHTY God and heavenly Father, of whose only gift it cometh that we can render unto thee acceptable service, sanctify our hearts, at this time, that we may worthily magnify thy holy Name. We thank thee that thou dost permit us to see the light of another day, and we beseech thee to continue to us thy merciful protection, and to bestow upon us whatever may be needful for our present and eternal welfare. Make us truly penitent for all our past transgressions, and enable us henceforth to be more watchful over ourselves, that we may escape from those sins which do most easily beset us. Help us to mortify and subdue the pride and wickedness of our hearts, and daily to proceed in all virtue and godliness of living. May we be humble in prosperity, and patient in adversity, submitting ourselves wholly to thy holy will and pleasure, and studying to serve thee in holiness and righteousness all the days of our life.

We beseech thee, O Lord, to bless and defend our rulers and our country. Continue to us the pure light of thy holy Gospel. Let there be peace and truth in our day: yea, let truth and justice, religion and piety, be established among us for all generations. Be gracious unto thy Church. Bless and prosper abundantly the ministers of thy holy Word. Bless them in their own souls, and make them a blessing to the souls of others. O Lord, increase the laborers in thy harvest, and fill the whole earth with the knowledge and love of Christ our Saviour.

Hear us, O Lord, in these our humble petitions; hear us for ourselves and for all whom we would remember before thee; hear us and be merciful unto us, and make the light of thy countenance to shine upon us; for the sake of Jesus Christ, our only Mediator and Advocate. *Amen.*

Our Father, who art in Heaven, &c.

The grace of our Lord Jesus Christ, &c.

Thursday Evening.

ALMIGHTY and everlasting God, who art of purer eyes than to behold iniquity, we draw near to thee under a deep sense of our unworthiness. We have sinned against thee in thought, word, and deed. Yet thou desirest not the death of a sinner; but rather that he should turn from his wickedness and live. Fulfil towards each of us those gracious promises which thou hast made in Jesus Christ: and enable us to rejoice in the sense of thy favor here, and in the hope of eternal life in the world to come.

And lest, through our own frailty, or the temptations which encompass us, we be drawn again into sin, vouchsafe us, we beseech thee, the constant direction and assistance of thy Holy Spirit. Put into our hearts good desires, and help us, by thy grace, to bring the same to good effect. Correct whatever is amiss in the temper and disposition of our souls, that no unholy thoughts, unlawful designs, or inordinate desires, may rest there. Purge our hearts from envy, hatred, and malice; that we may never suffer the sun to go down upon our wrath; but may always go to our rest in peace, charity, and good-will, with a conscience void of offence towards thee, and towards men: that so we may be preserved pure and blameless, unto the coming of our Lord and Saviour Jesus Christ.

May thy blessing, O Lord, rest upon us as a family. May our children be trained up in thy holy nurture. May they be kept, by thy grace, from the evils that are in the world, and early take upon themselves the solemn vows and promises of their Baptism, and at last be numbered among thy children in heaven. Bless all our relatives and friends. Be merciful to those who are in any trouble; and do thou, the God of pity, administer to them according to their several necessities. Let the light of thy Gospel shine upon all mankind. Have mercy on this land. Bless our President, and all others in authority.

Save us from the just consequences of our many and grievous sins, as a people, and help us to amend our ways, and to live according to thy laws. Give grace to all bishops and other ministers, that both by their preaching and living they may set forth thy word, and show it accordingly.

Into thy hands, O our heavenly Father, we now commend ourselves for this night. Thou hast mercifully preserved us through the day; and do thou continue unto us thy gracious protection; for Jesus Christ's sake. *Amen.*

Our Father who art in Heaven, &c.

The grace of our Lord Jesus Christ, &c.

Friday Morning.

O MOST mighty God and merciful Father, who hast compassion upon all men, and hatest nothing that thou hast made; we, thy needy and sinful creatures, would draw near to thee with reverence and godly fear, confessing our unworthiness, and imploring pardon and remission of our sins through the merits and intercession of thy dear Son. We bless thee that thou didst freely give him up for us all, and that he died, the just for the unjust, that he might bring us to God. Enable us, we beseech thee, this day and evermore, to keep in lively remembrance his most precious death and sacrifice. May we put our whole trust in his perfect atonement, and also daily endeavor ourselves to follow the blessed steps of his most holy life. May we imitate his great humility, his meekness and patience, his submission to thy will, and his delight in thy service. Casting away all self-righteousness, and reliance upon what we have done, may we receive him as the Lord our Righteousness, and depend upon him as our all in all.

And we beseech thee, O God, to extend the knowledge of the truth as it is in Jesus to all the families and people of the earth. Send forth more laborers into thy harvest, and let thy Gospel be preached among all nations. May the heathen be given to thy Son for his inheritance, and the uttermost parts of the earth for his possession. May he see of the travail of his soul, and be satisfied. And may we, thy servants, be ready to deny ourselves, that we may extend his kingdom, and glorify his blessed Name.

Direct and bless us this day in all our doings with thy most gracious favor, and preserve us from all evil and danger. Be gracious unto all our relatives, friends, and brethren. Let thy continual pity cleanse and defend thy Church. Endue thy ministers with holy zeal. Have compassion on the poor, the sick, and the afflicted. May the young be guided in thy holy ways. May all Israel be saved; and may the whole world be filled with thy glory.

All which we beg through him who died for our sins, and rose again for our justification, thy Son our Saviour Jesus Christ, to whom with thee, O Father, and thee, O Holy Ghost, be all honor and glory world without end. *Amen.*

Our Father, who art in Heaven, &c.

The grace of our Lord Jesus Christ, &c.,

Friday Evening.

O LORD our heavenly Father, by whose power and goodness we have been preserved this day; we bless thee for all thy mercies, temporal and spiritual, and we beseech thee to give us grace to show forth our thankfulness by an humble, holy, and obedient walking before thee all our days. May the close of this and every day remind us that all things are coming to an end. As faithful servants of Christ, our blessed Lord and Master, may we be always looking for his coming. Grant that it may be our blessedness to be found watching, and our reward to enter into thy eternal joy. In the hour of death, and in the day of judgment, good Lord, deliver us.

We again commend ourselves, O God, to thy care and protection. May we abide this night under the shadow of thy wings; and should we arise in the morning, to enter again upon the duties and cares of this life, may thy fear and love dwell in our hearts, and influence all our doings. May thy grace and mercy preserve us from every evil way, and enable us so to pass through things temporal, that we finally lose not the things eternal.

Give thy blessing, O Lord, to our rulers, and let it rest abundantly on our country. Save us from the judgments which we deserve by our sins, and give us that righteousness which exalteth a nation. Bless thy

Church universal, and prosper every effort for its extension among all mankind. Give success to the ministers and stewards of thy mysteries, and send forth more laborers into thy harvest. Be gracious to our dear relations and friends, and make them to be numbered with thy saints in glory everlasting. Be merciful to all who are in sorrow, need, sickness, or any other adversity, and grant them thy heavenly consolations.

All which we humbly beg through Jesus Christ, our most blessed Lord and Saviour. *Amen.*

Our Father, who art in Heaven, &c.

The grace of our Lord Jesus Christ, &c.

Saturday Morning.

ALMIGHTY and most merciful God, thou hast spared us to see the light of another day.

May we approach thy throne, rejoicing in thee, and ascribing all our salvation to thee.

We thank thee, O Lord, for all thy mercies renewed to us this morning. May they increase in us a renewed sense of thy love to our souls. Draw out our desires after thee, and fix our affections upon thee. May we begin the day in thy strength, pass through it in thy fear and love, and end it to thy glory.

Be with us, we beseech thee, to bless and uphold our souls. Grant us the joy of faith, the patience of hope, and the comfort of love. Save and deliver us from every evil, and cause all things to work together for our good. Compass us about with thy favor as with a shield. Let thy loving-kindness and truth always preserve us.

Make us diligent, we pray thee, in the discharge of our temporal and spiritual duties. Incline us so to seek thy kingdom and righteousness, that all other things may be added unto us. Give us grace to set an infinite value upon our souls. In the midst of life, may we think on death, judgment, and eternity; and may we give all diligence to be found of Christ in peace with God, without spot and blameless.

May thy blessing, O God, rest upon us as a family. May our children be thy children, partakers of thy grace, and heirs of thy heavenly kingdom. Bless all our relatives and friends. May they enjoy thy favor in this life, and at last enter into thy eternal joy. Have pity upon the poor, the sick, and the sorrowful. Bind up the broken-hearted; relieve the oppressed; be a Father to the fatherless, and the widow's God; and hasten on the time when all mankind shall know thy truth, and rejoice in thy salvation.

Pardon, O Lord, our manifold sins, and accept these our prayers, in the name and through the merits of Jesus Christ, our blessed Saviour and Redeemer. *Amen.*

Our Father, who art in Heaven, &c.

The grace of our Lord Jesus Christ, &c.

Saturday Evening.

O ALMIGHTY Lord and everlasting God, unto whom all hearts are open, all desires known, and from whom no secrets are hid; cleanse the thoughts of our hearts by the inspiration of thy Holy Spirit, that the worship which we now offer may please thee, and that the rest of our life hereafter may be pure and holy in thy sight. By thy gracious protection we have been carried through another day and another week, and we would render thee our humble and hearty thanks for all thy goodness and loving-kindness. But, O God, we have rebelled against thee in the midst of all thy mercies. We have broken thy laws, and resisted the influences of thy Holy Spirit. Create and make in us new and contrite hearts; that we, worthily lamenting our sins, and acknowledging our wretchedness, may obtain of thee, the God of all mercy, perfect remission and forgiveness, through Jesus Christ. Give us the comforting assurance of pardon, and lift upon us the light of thy countenance. O God, make us more and more holy. May we be complete in Christ, and may his love constrain us in all our works and ways. May we cling to his cross, and live to his glory.

Preserve us, O Lord, through the night, and bring us in safety to the light of another day; and as that day is more especially thine, prepare us to sanctify and use it to the profit of our souls. May thy blessing rest upon all with whom we are united in the bonds of kindred or affection, and may they be thine here and for ever.

Bless thy Church universal, and especially that portion of it to which we belong. May the labors of thy ministering servants be crowned with success. Give them wisdom and zeal. Fill them with love, and clothe them with humility. O thou Lord of the harvest, send forth more laborers into thy harvest, and fill the whole earth with thy glory.

Give thy blessing, O Lord, to our civil rulers, and to our whole country. Save us from thy merited displeasure, and make us to be a nation fearing thee, and working righteousness. And wilt thou hasten the time when all the kingdoms of this world shall become the kingdoms of our Lord and of his Christ; through the same, Jesus Christ thy Son, our Saviour and Redeemer. *Amen.*

Our Father, who art in Heaven, Hallowed be thy Name. Thy Kingdom come. Thy Will be done on Earth, as it is in Heaven. Give us this day our daily bread. And forgive us our trespasses, As we forgive those who trespass against us. And lead us not into temptation; But deliver us from evil: For thine is the kingdom, and the power, and the glory, for ever and ever. Amen.

The grace of our Lord Jesus Christ, and the love of God, and the fellowship of the Holy Ghost, be with us all evermore. *Amen.*

OCCASIONAL AND PRIVATE PRAYERS.

Christmas Day.

ALMIGHTY GOD, the Father of our Lord Jesus Christ, we humbly beseech thee, for his sake, to accept our hearty thanks for the manifold mercies which thou hast, poured upon us.

We bless thee, especially, for sending, as on this day, thy well-beloved Son, to take our nature upon him, and to be made in the likeness of sinful flesh. And we would join the multitude of the heavenly host in praising thee, and saying, Glory to God in the highest, on earth peace, good will toward men.

And as, when thou didst bring thy first-begotten into the world, thou didst command all the heavenly host to worship him, so may we also give unto him the glory which is due unto his name.

Be with us, O Lord, in all the duties and enjoyments of this day. As children of Sion, may we be joyful in our King; and may we show forth his praise in an humble and obedient walking before him all the days of our life. Assist us in duly observing this sacred season; and grant that we may ever account it a faithful saying, and worthy of all acceptation, that Christ Jesus came into the world to save sinners.

May the glad tidings which we this day commemorate be speedily made known unto all people; so that from the rising of the sun, even unto the going down of the same, the name of Jesus may be great among the Gentiles, and in every place incense and a pure offering be offered unto his name. In him may the Gentiles trust, and find his rest to be glorious.

Have compassion, O God, upon thine ancient people Israel. Take from them all ignorance, pride, and prejudice, and bring them to an acknowledgment of the truth as it is in Jesus.

Regard with thy favor all who profess and

call themselves Christians. May they be so joined together in unity of spirit, and in the bond of peace, that they may be a holy temple acceptable unto thee.

And as at thy first coming, O Lord Jesus Christ, thou didst send thy messenger to prepare thy way before thee, we beseech thee to grant that the ministers and stewards of thy mysteries, may likewise so prepare and make ready thy way, by turning the hearts of the disobedient to the wisdom of the just, that, at thy second coming to judge the world, we may be found an acceptable people in thy sight, who livest and reignest with the Father and the Holy Spirit, ever one God, world without end. • *Amen.*

Our Father, who art in Heaven, &c.

The grace of our Lord Jesus Christ, &c.

The Beginning or Close of a Year.*

ADORABLE and ever-gracious God, whose days are without end, and whose mercies cannot be numbered, thou art from everlasting to everlasting the same, yesterday, to-day, and for ever. Thou hast laid the foundation of the earth, and the heavens are the work of thy hands. They shall perish, but thou remainest: they all shall wax old as doth a garment, and shall be changed; but thou art the same, and thy years shall not fail. Though days and months and years do pass away, and time itself shall be no longer, thy kingdom shall endure for ever and ever.

Behold in mercy thy needy, dependent, and perishing creatures, whose life is but a span, and whose age is even as nothing in respect of thee. It is of thy mercy that we are not consumed, and because thy compassions fail not. Thou holdest our souls in life,

* By Bishop Griswold.

and to thee we lift our eyes as the only hope of all the ends of the earth.

We thank thee, O blessed Lord God, that while another year has [nearly] passed away, and thousands and tens of thousands of precious souls have departed to the eternal world, we yet survive; that we have been, by thy merciful providence, conducted through innumerable perils to this present time.

Help us, O heavenly Father, so to number our days, and so duly to consider the shortness and uncertainty of human life, that we may apply our hearts to true wisdom. Shouldst thou, O Lord, in thy goodness, let us alone another year also, give us grace, we beseech thee, to serve thee better than in times past. Create us again unto good works, and renew us day by day. Our life and breath are thine; our times are in thy hand; and may our whole heart and soul be devoted unto thee, and we be ever prepared to say, To live is Christ, and to die is gain. Support us in all dangers, both of soul and body. Lead us not into temptation; but deliver us from evil.

We ask it in the name, and through the mediation of our Lord and Saviour Jesus Christ. *Amen.*

Our Father, who art in Heaven, &c.

The grace of our Lord Jesus Christ, &c.

Epiphany.

A PRAYER FOR MISSIONS.

O GOD, who by the leading of a star didst manifest thy only-begotten Son to the Gentiles, give us hearts, we beseech thee, to be duly thankful for this thine unspeakable goodness, and hear our supplications and prayers. May a thankful sense of thy mercy to our fallen, sinful race, awaken in our hearts a deep concern for the salvation of those for whom the Saviour died. Give thy blessing, we beseech thee, to the means and efforts used for the spreading abroad of the

Gospel, and for extending the light of thy word through the darkness of this sinful world.

Accept, O Lord, our supplications for those nations and people of the earth who are sitting in the shadow of death, having no hope, and without God in the world; and for all who are in error, or ignorance, or unbelief. May the Sun of Righteousness rise upon them with healing in his wings, and may they rejoice in his salvation. Bless thy word wherever it is spoken, and send it where it is not heard. May it be truly preached, truly received, and truly followed, and the whole earth be speedily filled with the knowledge of the Lord.

Let thy blessing rest, O God, upon the ministers of thy Gospel; and especially upon those who are laboring in heathen lands to build up the Redeemer's kingdom. Preserve them from perils by land, and perils by water, from sickness, from the violence of enemies, and from every evil to which they may be exposed. May they be instruments of turning many to righteousness, and hereafter shine as the brightness of the firmament, and as the stars, for ever and ever.

Make us ready, O Lord, to give according to our ability for the promotion of this great work, and may we rejoice in every opportunity of laboring together with thee for the extension of thy Church among all nations and people.

Hear us in these our prayers, and hasten on the time when thy name and thy praise shall be spread abroad in all the world, and when all shall know and love and serve thee from the least even unto the greatest; through thine infinite mercy in Jesus Christ, our most blessed Lord and Saviour. *Amen.*

Our Father, who art in Heaven, &c.

The grace of our Lord Jesus Christ, &c.

Ash-Wednesday.

ALMIGHTY and everlasting God, who hatest nothing that thou hast made, and dost forgive the sins of all those who are penitent; create and make in us new and contrite hearts, that we, worthily lamenting our sins, and acknowledging our wretchedness, may obtain of thee, the God of all mercy, perfect remission and forgiveness; through Jesus Christ our Lord.

Thy property is always to have mercy; to thee only it appertaineth to forgive sins; spare us, therefore, good Lord, spare thy people, whom thou hast redeemed: enter not into judgment with thy servants, who are vile earth, and miserable sinners, but turn thine anger from us, and absolve us from our offences.

May the solemn season on which we have this day entered be to us a time of refreshing from thy presence, and of mercy to our souls. May we humble ourselves as in dust and ashes, meekly acknowledging our vileness, and truly repenting us of our faults. O make us to hear of joy and gladness, that the bones which thou hast broken may rejoice. Turn thou us, O good Lord, and so shall we be turned, and after the multitude of thy mercies look upon us, and be gracious unto us.

Bless thy people, O Lord, and blot out all their transgressions. Be with them in all the duties and services of this season of humiliation, and may they so fast and pray as to offer unto thee an acceptable sacrifice through thy dear Son. Strengthen thy ministering servants for all the duties of their sacred office, and make them wise in winning souls to Christ, and in building up thy people in their most holy faith.

Be with us, O Lord, this day, and all the days of our lives, and finally receive us in thy kingdom, through Jesus Christ our Saviour. *Amen.**

Our Father who art in Heaven, &c.

The grace of our Lord Jesus Christ, &c.

* With slight alterations, this prayer will be appropriate for Fasting days appointed by the Civil Authority.

Good-Friday.

O GOD, our heavenly Father, who of thy tender mercy didst give thine only Son, Jesus Christ, to suffer death upon the cross for our redemption, behold us this morning, we beseech thee, with favor and compassion, and may this day be a day of grace and mercy to our souls.

Make us deeply sensible of the sins which caused our blessed Redeemer to bleed and die, the just for the unjust, that he might bring us to thee. Raise us, we beseech thee, O heavenly Father, from the death of sin unto the life of righteousness. May we never by our transgressions crucify thy dear Son afresh; but may we sanctify the Lord God in our hearts, and live soberly, righteously, and godly, in this present world, through him who loved us and gave himself for us.

O Lord Jesus Christ, who, in love to us, miserable sinners, didst leave the glories of thy heavenly throne, and come into this world to put away sin by the sacrifice of thyself; who didst become a man of sorrows and acquainted with grief; and didst humble thyself and become obedient unto death, even the death of the cross; spare us, good Lord; spare those for whose sins thou didst vouchsafe to shed thine own precious blood. O Lord God, Lamb of God, Son of the Father, who takest away the sins of the world, have mercy upon us. Thou that takest away the sins of the world, receive our prayer. By thine agony and bloody sweat, by thy cross and passion, and by thy precious death, O Lord, deliver us, and save us for ever.

And we beseech thee, O God, to have compassion on a world lying in wickedness, for which our Lord Jesus Christ was contented to be betrayed, and given up into the hands of wicked men, and to suffer death upon the cross. We pray especially for those whose forefathers shed this innocent blood. Let it no longer be upon them and upon their children. Take from them an evil heart of unbelief. Pour down upon them the spirit of grace and supplication, that they may look upon him whom they have pierced, and believe on him who was born King of the Jews. May they no more be a proverb and a by-word among the nations, but be Israelites indeed, in whom is no guile.

Have mercy on all others who are enemies of the cross of Christ; to whom he is a stone of stumbling, and a rock of offence; and deliver them from the awful guilt of neglecting his great salvation.

Bless those who are appointed to preach thy glorious Gospel; and let them know nothing among men save Jesus Christ and him crucified.

Make thy chosen people joyful, glorying only in the cross of Christ, and living the life which they live in the flesh by faith in his blessed name.

And, finally, may it please thee that all the ends of the earth may look unto Christ, and be saved for ever.

Grant this, for the sake of the same, thy

Son Jesus Christ, our only Mediator and Advocate. *Amen.*

Our Father, who art in Heaven, &c.

The grace of our Lord Jesus Christ, &c.

Easter Day.

O MERCIFUL God, the Father of our Lord Jesus Christ, who was dead, and is alive again, we rejoice in the return of this sacred day, on which he loosed the pains of death, and arose from the grave, being made the first-fruits of them that slept.

We bless thee that he was delivered for our offences, and raised again for our justification; and may it please thee, O Lord God, the God of peace, who didst bring from the dead the Lord Jesus Christ, the great shepherd of the sheep, through the blood of the everlasting covenant, to make us perfect in every good word and work, to do thy will, working in us that which is well-pleasing in thy sight.

O thou, who art the Resurrection and the Life, raise us, we beseech thee, from the death of sin unto the life of righteousness. Quicken us in all the duties of this day. Since thou hast been sacrificed for us, may we keep the feast, and be joyful in thy house of prayer. [Give us grace to approach thy holy table with penitence and faith, offering ourselves, and all that we have, and all that we are, as a reasonable, holy, and living sacrifice unto thee.]

Pour down thy Spirit, O God, on the ministers of thy blessed Gospel, [especially thy servant who is our own spiritual pastor and guide.] While they preach Jesus and the resurrection, let thy word in their mouth be as life from the dead; that so they who are sleeping in their sins may awake and arise from the dead, that Christ may give them life.

And grant us grace, O Lord, to consider that the hour is coming in which all that are in the graves shall come forth; and O may we have part in the first resurrection, and a seat among the redeemed in glory everlasting, through Jesus Christ, our only Mediator and Redeemer. *Amen.*

Our Father, who art in Heaven, &c.

The grace of our Lord Jesus Christ, &c.

Ascension Day.*

O GOD, the King of glory, who hast exalted thine only Son Jesus Christ, with great triumph unto thy kingdom in heaven; we beseech thee, leave us not comfortless; but send to us thine Holy Ghost to comfort us, and exalt us unto the same place whither our Saviour Christ is gone before; and grant that like as we do believe him to have ascended into the heavens; so we may also in heart and mind thither ascend, and with him

* To be used with the prayer for the morning and evening.

continually dwell. May our affections be set on things above, and not on things on the earth. May our life be hid with Christ in God; and when Christ, who is our life, shall appear, may we also appear with him in glory; that where he is, there we may be also. May we continually remember that this same Jesus, who was taken up into heaven, will so come in like manner as he went up into heaven; and oh, when he shall come again, in his glorious majesty, to judge both the quick and dead, may we rise to the life immortal, and reign with him in his kingdom world without end. *Amen.*

Whit-Sunday.

O GOD, who as at this time didst teach the hearts of thy faithful people, by sending to them the light of thy Holy Spirit, we bless and praise thy holy name for this wonderful manifestation of thy goodness and tender mercy.

With the light of this holy day lift upon us the light of thy countenance, and grant that thy Holy Spirit may give us a right judgment in all things. May He ever be with us as a Spirit of wisdom and understanding; a Spirit of counsel and strength; a Spirit of knowledge and true godliness; a Spirit of reverence and holy fear; a Spirit of truth, love, and unity; a Spirit of everlasting consolation. Direct us in all the duties and solemnities of this day, and help us to worship thee, who art a Spirit, in spirit and in truth. May we be in the Spirit on the Lord's day, and devoutly offer before thee the incense of prayer and praise in the congregation of thy people.

O God, Holy Ghost, Sanctifier of the faithful, visit us, we pray thee, with thy love and favor; enlighten our minds more and more with the light of the everlasting Gospel; graft in our hearts a love of the truth; increase in us true religion; nourish us with all goodness; and of thy great mercy keep us in the same.

And, O Lord, wilt thou extend the riches

of thy grace to all thy people. Pour out thy Spirit upon all flesh. Send out thy light and thy truth to the nations that have never heard thy name. May they soon hear thy ministering servants speaking in their own tongues the wonderful works of God. Look with pity on thine ancient people Israel. By the power of the Holy Ghost may both Jews and Gentiles be converted to Christ, and every tongue confess that he is Lord, to the glory of God the Father.

Give grace, O heavenly Father, to all the bishops and pastors of thy Church. Make them diligent and faithful in the work to which the Holy Ghost has called them, to the glory of thy great Name, and the edification of the people committed to their charge. [Bless him, especially, who is appointed to offer the sacrifices of prayer and praise in the congregation to which we belong. May the words of his mouth, and the meditation of his heart, be always acceptable in thy sight. May thy Spirit be with him as a Comforter and Guide, and at last may he enter into the joy of his Lord.]

We offer these our supplications and prayers in the name of Jesus Christ our Saviour, to whom, with thee, O Father, and thee, O Holy Ghost, be ascribed equal adoration and praise, now and evermore. *Amen.*

Our Father, who art in Heaven, &c.

The grace of our Lord Jesus Christ, &c.

Trinity Sunday.*

WE praise thee, O God, we acknowledge thee to be the Lord. All the earth doth worship thee, the Father everlasting. To thee all angels cry aloud, the heavens, and all the powers therein. Heaven and earth are full of the majesty of thy glory. The Holy Church, throughout all the world, doth acknowledge thee; the Father, of an infinite

* To be used in connection with the prayer for Sunday Morning and Evening.

majesty; thine adorable, true, and only Son; also, the Holy Ghost, the Comforter.

O holy, blessed, and glorious Trinity, three Persons and one God, have mercy upon us, miserable sinners. And as thou, O God, hast given unto us thy servants grace, by the confession of a true faith, to acknowledge the glory of the eternal Trinity, and in the power of the Divine Majesty to worship the Unity; we beseech thee that thou wouldest keep us steadfast in this faith, and evermore defend us from all adversities, who livest and reignest, one God, world without end. *Amen.*

The Fourth Day of July.

O LORD GOD, the King of kings, and Lord of lords, who dost from thy throne behold and govern all the nations of the earth, we bless thee on this day for all thy mercies to the good land which thou hast given us. We adore thee as the God in whom our fathers trusted, and by whose goodness we have been preserved through many and great perils till the present time. May the return of this day call to our remembrance thy mercies which have ever been of old; and may we seek that righteousness which exalteth a nation, and avoid those sins which are a reproach to any people, and which will expose us to thy just wrath and indignation.

Bless thy servant, the President of the United States, and all others in authority; and so replenish them with the grace of thy Holy Spirit, that they may always incline to thy will, and walk in thy way. Bless all the people of our land. O be thou our shield and buckler, that we, surely trusting in thy defence, may not fear the power of any adversaries. Continue thy merciful goodness to us and to our country. Give us unity, peace, and concord. Preserve us from strife and contention, and from all those judgments which our sins are calling down upon us; and may we ever be that happy people whose God is the Lord.

Extend, O Lord, the blessings which we

enjoy to all the nations of the earth. May light and liberty be more and more spread abroad, till all the kingdoms of this world shall become the kingdoms of our Lord and Saviour Jesus Christ. May the time soon come when the nations shall learn war no more, when all tyranny and oppression shall cease, and the knowledge of the Lord fill the earth as the waters cover the sea.

Let thy good providence, O Lord, be over us and around us this day. Preserve us from every danger to which we may be exposed, and grant that all our doings, being ordered by thy governance, may be righteous in thy sight. Bless all who are near and dear to us, granting them, in this world, knowledge of thy truth, and in the world to come life everlasting.

We offer these our thanksgivings and prayers in the name and through the merits of Jesus Christ our Lord. *Amen.*

Our Father, who art in Heaven, &c.

The grace of our Lord Jesus Christ, &c.

A Prayer for our Country,

TO BE USED AT DISCRETION WITH THE DAILY PRAYERS.

WE beseech thee, O Lord, to look in mercy upon our country, and make us to be a nation fearing thee and working righteousness. May our Rulers be under thy special care and protection. May they incline to thy will, and walk in thy way. And may all the people enjoy thy heavenly benediction, and dwell securely under the shadow of thy wings. May they submit to every ordinance of man for the Lord's sake, and be evermore preserved from the sins of sedition, privy conspiracy, and rebellion. Give peace in our time, O Lord; and may liberty, unity, and concord ever prevail throughout our borders. May we have that righteousness which exalteth a nation, and be that happy people whose God is the Lord. May we put our whole trust in thy holy arm; and wilt thou make it appear that thou, who wast the God of our fathers, art our Saviour and mighty Deliverer throughout all generations, through Jesus Christ our Lord. *Amen.*

Thanksgiving Day.

O ALMIGHTY LORD and everlasting God, by whose mercy we are again permitted to present the annual tribute of our thanks and praise; we bless thee for all thy goodness and loving-kindness to us and to all men.

By thy wisdom, O Lord, thou hast founded the earth; by thy understanding hast thou established the heavens; by thy knowledge the depths are broken up, and the clouds drop down the dew. We bless thee for the returns of seed-time and harvest, and for crowning the year with the bounties of thy providence. Thou makest thy sun to rise on the evil and on the good, and sendest rain on the just and on the unjust.

We praise thee for thy mercies to us as a family and household, beseeching thee to continue thy goodness to us, and enable us to show our thankfulness by an humble and obedient walking before thee all our days. Bless all who are near and dear to us, wherever, in thy providence, they may be. May grace, mercy, and peace be upon them, and may they at last be received into thy heavenly kingdom.

Bless, O Lord, all the people of this land. Pour down upon them the spirit of unfeigned gratitude and love for all thy mercies. May they enter thy gates with thanksgiving, and thy courts with praise. May they honor thee with their substance, and with the first-fruits of all their increase. May they depart from all iniquity, and acknowledge thee as the Lord their God. Bless all who are in authority over us, and may they rule in thy fear, and as those who must give account.

Be merciful, O God, to the poor and needy. May we rejoice with those that do rejoice, and weep with those that weep. Fill our hearts with tenderness and compassion toward the distressed and afflicted, the widow and the fatherless, and may we remember the words of the Lord Jesus, how he said, It is more blessed to give than to receive. May portions be sent to those for whom nothing is prepared, and may all rejoice in thy goodness, and give thanks unto thy holy Name.

Assist us, O Lord, in all the duties of this day. Sanctify to us our domestic enjoyments and our public privileges, and make us duly thankful for all our temporal and spiritual blessings. Pardon our manifold sins, and finally save us in glory everlasting, for Jesus' sake. *Amen.*

Our Father, who art in Heaven, &c.

The grace of our Lord Jesus Christ, &c.

A Prayer

IN TIME OF PUBLIC DANGERS OR TROUBLES.*

O most mighty God! King of kings, and Lord of lords, without whose care the watchman waketh but in vain, we implore, in this our time of need, thy succor and blessing in behalf of our rulers and magistrates, and of all the people of this land, (*or*, of this commonwealth, *or*, of this community.) Remember not our many and great transgressions; turn from us the judgments which we feel or fear; and give us wisdom to discern, and courage to attempt, and faithfulness to do, and patience to endure, whatsoever shall be well-pleasing in thy sight; that so thy chastenings may yield the peaceable fruits of righteousness, and that at the last we may rejoice in thy salvation, through Jesus Christ our Lord. *Amen.*

* To be used with the Daily Prayers.

A Thanksgiving

FOR DELIVERANCE FROM PUBLIC CALAMITIES.*

O Eternal God, the shield of our help, beneath whose sovereign defence thy people dwell in safety, we bless and praise, we laud and magnify thy glorious name for all thy goodness to the people of this land, (*or*, of this commonwealth, *or*, of this community,) and especially for our merciful deliverance from those calamities which of late we suffered, (*or*, dreaded.) Inspire our souls with grateful love; lift up our voices in songs of thankfulness; and so pour out upon us thy Holy Spirit, that we may be humble and watchful in our prosperity, patient and steadfast in our afflictions, and always enjoy the blessed confidence of that people whose God is the Lord; all which we ask through Jesus Christ, our Mediator and Redeemer, to whom,

* To be used with the Daily Prayers.

with the Father and the Holy Ghost, be all honor and glory, praise and dominion, now and for ever. *Amen.*

Prayer for the Minister.

O ALMIGHTY GOD, who, of thy wise providence, hast appointed divers orders of ministers in thy Church, give thy grace, we humbly beseech thee, to thy servant who is our appointed teacher and guide in holy things. Wilt thou rule his heart, strengthen his hands, and bless his labors. Endue him with every gift and grace necessary to the full and faithful performance of all the duties of his office. Awaken in his mind a holy zeal for thy glory, and for the salvation of souls. Help him to devote himself, and all his powers and faculties, to the great work to which he is called. Enlighten his mind with the truths of thy word, and with the doctrines of eternal life. Be ever with him in the discharge of his sacred duties. Support him under every discouragement. Comfort him with success in his labors. Remove from him all fear of man; and give him utterance that he may open his mouth boldly to make known the mystery of the Gospel, and to declare all the counsel of God.

And wilt thou, O Lord, watch over him for good. May his life and health be precious in thy sight. Bless him [in his family] in his private studies, and in his public ministrations. May he be instrumental in turning many to righteousness; and at last, having fought a good fight, and finished his course with joy, may he receive a crown of righteousness in thy kingdom and glory on high.

And give us grace, O Lord, we beseech thee, rightly and duly to profit by his ministry, and to do all in our power to aid and encourage him in the arduous duties of his office. Attending diligently upon his ministrations, may we receive with meekness the engrafted word which is able to save our souls, and search the Scriptures daily, to know the certainty of those things wherein we are instructed. May he be ready, with all faithful diligence, to banish and drive away from the Church all erroneous and strange doctrines contrary to thy Word, and maintain, in all its purity and power, the truth as it is in Jesus, knowing nothing among us save Jesus Christ and him crucified.

And thus may both minister and people be finally received into the general assembly and Church of the first-born, whose names are written in heaven; through the merits and mediation of Jesus Christ our Saviour. *Amen.*

Our Father, who art in Heaven, &c.

The grace of our Lord Jesus Christ, &c.

A Minister's Prayer

FOR HIMSELF AND HIS PEOPLE.

O LORD my God! I am not worthy that thou shouldest come under my roof; yet thou hast honored thy servant with appointing him to stand in thy House, and to serve at thy Holy Altar. To thee and to thy service I devote myself, soul, body, and spirit — with all their powers and faculties. Fill my memory with the words of thy law; enlighten my understanding with the illumination of the Holy Ghost; and may all the wishes and desires of my will centre in what thou hast commanded. And, to make me instrumental in promoting the salvation of the people committed to my charge, grant that I may faithfully administer thy holy Sacraments, and by my life and doctrine set forth thy true and lively Word. Be ever with me in the performance of all the duties of my ministry: in prayer, to quicken my devotion;

in praises, to heighten my love and gratitude; and in preaching, to give a readiness of thought and expression suitable to the clearness and excellency of thy Holy Word. May I determine to know nothing among men save Jesus Christ and him crucified, and may I faithfully declare all the counsel of God. Help me, O Lord, to keep my own heart with all diligence, and to walk closely with thee in all holy conversation and godliness. May I be sincere and honest in my ministry, not walking in craftiness, nor handling thy Word deceitfully, but by manifestation of the truth may I commend myself to every man's conscience in thy sight. And wilt thou, O God, bless thy Word spoken by my mouth, and give it such success that it may never be spoken in vain. May the impenitent be awakened; may the young be guided in the right way; and may thy people daily proceed in all virtue and godliness of living. May I realize more and more the solemn responsibilities of my holy office, and ever keep in mind that I must render unto thee a strict account of my stewardship. Oh may I be a faithful laborer in thy vineyard, — faithful as a pastor of the flock, and as a teacher of thy Word. May I be faithful to my own soul, and to the souls of my people. May my life be hid with Christ in God; so that when Christ, who is my life, shall appear, I may also appear with him in glory. Grant this for the sake of Jesus Christ, thy Son, our Saviour. *Amen.*

Prayer

FOR AN INCREASE OF LABORERS IN THE LORD'S VINEYARD.

ALMIGHTY and everlasting God, who by thy Son Jesus Christ didst give commandment to the holy Apostles, that they should go into all the world and preach the Gospel to every creature; give us, we beseech thee, a ready will to obey thy Word, and fill us with a hearty desire to make thy way known upon earth, thy saving health among all nations.

Look with pity and compassion upon the heathen that have not known thee, and upon the multitudes in our own land that are scattered abroad as sheep having no shepherd. Regard with thy favor and blessing every effort to increase the number of those who are ministers of Christ, and stewards of the mysteries of God. O Thou Lord of the harvest, hear our prayers and supplications, and send forth laborers into thy harvest. Incline the hearts of the young to remember thee, their Creator, in the days of their youth, and to give themselves up to thy service in the ministry of reconciliation. Raise up, we pray thee, a great company of preachers, and prepare them by thy grace for their high and holy calling. Replenish them with the truth of thy doctrine, and endue them with innocency of life, that they may faithfully serve before thee, to the glory of thy great name, and the benefit of thy holy Church. By their labor and ministry may they gather together a great flock in all the parts of the world; and so spread abroad thy Gospel, that the whole of thy dispersed sheep, being gathered into one fold, shall become partakers of everlasting life; through the merits and death of Jesus Christ our Saviour. *Amen.*

Prayer

FOR A BLESSING ON THE DIOCESE.

O GOD, Holy Ghost, Sanctifier of the faithful, visit, we pray thee, this Diocese with thy love and favor. Enlighten the minds of our ministers and people with the light of the everlasting Gospel. Give to our Bishop a holy zeal in thy service, and sustain him in all his labors and trials. May we all be so joined together in unity of spirit, and in the bond of peace, that we may be an holy temple acceptable unto thee. Help us in every effort to extend the borders of Sion, and to build up the Redeemer's kingdom. May we know nothing in our labors save Jesus Christ, and his blessed Gospel'; and may we be builded together on the true foundation, as an habitation of God through thee. May faithful ministers of Jesus Christ be increased in our midst; so that the wilderness and the solitary place shall be glad for them, and the desert rejoice and blossom as the rose. Graft in our hearts a love of the truth; increase in us true religion; nourish us with all goodness; and of thy great mercy keep us in the same, O blessed Spirit, whom, with the Father and the Son together, we worship and glorify as one God, world without end. *Amen.*

Prayer

FOR UNITY AMONG ALL CHRISTIAN PEOPLE.

O GOD, the Father of our Lord Jesus Christ, our only Saviour, the Prince of Peace, give us grace to desire the prosperity of thy holy Church universal, and to set forwards, as much as lieth in us, quietness, peace, and love, among all Christian people. May we seriously lay to heart the great dangers we are in by our unhappy divisions. Take away all hatred and prejudice, and whatsoever else may hinder thy people from godly union and concord : that as there is but one Body, and one Spirit, and one Hope of our calling, one Lord, one Faith, one Baptism, one God and Father of us all; so may we henceforth be all of one heart, and of one soul, united in one holy bond of Truth and Peace, of Faith and Charity, and may with one mind and one mouth glorify thee, our heavenly Father, ever praying that thy grace may be with all them that love our Lord Jesus Christ in sincerity. And grant that the course of this world may be so peaceably ordered by thy governance, that thy Church may joyfully serve thee in all godly quietness; that so they may walk in the ways of Truth and Peace, and finally be numbered with thy Saints in glory everlasting; through thy merits, O blessed Jesus, thou gracious Bishop and Shepherd of our souls, who art with the Father and the Holy Ghost, one God, world without end. *Amen.*

A Bishop's Prayer

FOR HIMSELF AND HIS DIOCESE.

O GOD, the strength of all who trust in thee, in a deep sense of my own weakness, and of that great charge which lies upon me, I come to thee for that heavenly grace which is sufficient for every time of need; and wilt thou have mercy upon me, and hearken unto my prayer. Called to the office and work of a Bishop in thy Church, may I have strength and power faithfully to perform the duties of my high calling, and to fulfil the solemn vows which rest upon me. May I faithfully exercise myself in the Holy Scriptures, and call upon thee for the true understanding of the same. May I be ready, with all faithful diligence, to banish and drive away from the Church all erroneous and strange doctrine contrary to thy Word, and encourage others to the same. May I deny all ungodliness and worldly lusts, and live soberly, righteously, and godly in this present world. May I maintain and set forward quietness, love, and peace among all men; and may I diligently exercise such discipline as by the authority of thy Word, and by the order of the Church, is committed unto me. May I be faithful in ordaining, sending, or laying hands upon others. May I be gentle and merciful, for Christ's sake, to poor and needy people, and to all strangers destitute of help. May I be humble and prayerful. May I be faithful to my own soul, and to the souls of those committed to my care; and grant that, by a diligent discharge of every duty, I may truly profit both the clergy and the people over whom I am placed in thy Name. Sustain me by thy Holy Spirit in every difficulty and trial, and help me to be watchful in all things, to endure afflictions, to do the work of an evangelist, and to make full proof of my ministry. Bless me in my studies, that I may faithfully preach thy Word, and be instrumental in converting many to the truth.

Give me wisdom and prudence and love, that I may not hinder thy Gospel; that I may rule in thy fear, and be patient towards all who oppose themselves. O Lord, bless the ministers of my Diocese, and make them wise in winning souls to Christ. May they declare all thy counsel, and live to thy glory. O Thou Lord of the harvest, send forth more laborers into thy harvest. Raise up faithful heralds of the cross, that the Gospel may be preached to every creature, and that a great flock may be gathered together in all the parts of the world, to set forth the eternal praise of thy holy name. Bless every member of this Diocese, and all thy people throughout the world. Bless me, O Lord, even me also, O my God. Bless me in my visitations, and in all my work. May I be willing to be the servant of all, that I may save some. Keep me, O Lord, from temptation and from sin. May I live near to the cross, and may Jesus, my Saviour, be my all in all. May I be a wholesome example to such as believe, and to all men, in word, in conversation, in love, in faith, in chastity, and in purity ; that faithfully fulfilling my course, at the latter day I may receive the crown of righteousness, laid up by the Lord, the righteous Judge, who liveth and reigneth one God, with the Father and the Holy Ghost, world without end. *Amen.*

Before Communion.*

GRANT us grace, O heavenly Father, to prepare our hearts for a due reception of the holy sacrament of the Lord's Supper. May we truly and earnestly repent of our sins. May we cherish a spirit of love and charity towards our neighbors. May we resolve, by thy help, to lead a new life, following thy commandments, and walking from henceforth in thy holy ways. As we show forth the death of our Saviour Christ, may we feed upon him in our hearts by faith, obtaining

* To be used with the prayer for the day.

remission of our sins, and all other benefits of his passion. May we dwell in him, and he in us, and may thy Spirit bear witness with our spirit that we are his true disciples. Save us, we beseech thee, from eating and drinking unworthily. May we judge ourselves, that we be not judged of the Lord. Sensible of our sinfulness and unworthiness, may we lay hold on the gracious invitations and promises of the Gospel, and then draw near with faith, receiving that holy sacrament to our comfort; that thus we may grow in grace and in the knowledge of our Lord and Saviour Jesus Christ.

Private Prayer before Communion.

ALMIGHTY and everlasting God, who of thy great and tender mercy didst give thine only Son Jesus Christ to suffer death upon the cross for our redemption, and hast instituted and ordained holy mysteries as pledges of his love, and for a continual remembrance of his death and passion, to our great and endless comfort; I beseech thee to give me grace to be duly thankful for this thine inestimable benefit, and to put my whole trust and confidence in this thy mercy so wonderfully manifested in thine unspeakable gift. And grant, O Lord, that I may this day most gratefully remember the exceeding love of my only Saviour Jesus Christ, thus dying for me; and work in me all such holy and heavenly affections, as may make me a worthy partaker of that holy table, prepared for the continual remembrance of the sacrifice of the death of Christ, and of those benefits which I receive thereby.

I do not presume to go to thy table, O merciful Lord, trusting in my own righteousness, but in thy manifold and great mercies. I am not worthy to gather up the crumbs under thy table. But thou art the same Lord, whose property is always to have mercy: grant me therefore, gracious Lord, so to eat the flesh of thy dear Son Jesus Christ, and to drink his blood, that my sinful body may be made clean by his body, and my soul washed through his most precious blood, and that I may evermore dwell in him and he in me.

And grant, O Lord, that I, and all who shall unite with me this day in this holy service, may be fed with the spiritual food of the most precious body and blood of thy Son our Saviour Jesus Christ; and be assured of thy favor and goodness towards us; and that we are very members incorporate in the mystical body of thy Son, which is the blessed company of all faithful people; and are also heirs through hope of thy everlasting kingdom, by the merits of the most precious death and passion of thy dear Son.

And now, O Lord, the only begotten Son Jesus Christ; O Lord God, Lamb of God, Son of the Father, that takest away the sins of the world, have mercy upon me. Thou that takest away the sins of the world, have mercy upon me. Thou that takest away the sins of the world, receive my prayer. Thou that sittest at the right hand of God the Father, have mercy upon me.

And here I offer and present unto thee, O Lord, my soul and body, to be a reasonable, holy, and living sacrifice unto thee, humbly beseeching thee that I and all who are partakers of this Holy Communion may be filled with thy grace and heavenly benediction. May I be crucified unto the world, and the world unto me; and may I live the life which I live in the flesh by the faith of the Son of God, who loved me and gave himself for me. Hear me, O Lord, and have mercy upon me, a miserable offender. And although I am unworthy, through my manifold sins, to offer unto thee any sacrifice, yet I beseech thee to accept this my bounden duty and service; not weighing my merits, but pardoning my offences, through Jesus Christ our Lord; by whom, and with whom, in the unity of the Holy Ghost, all honor and glory be unto thee, O Father Almighty, world without end. *Amen.*

For a Birth-day.*

O God, heavenly Father, who hast been graciously pleased to prolong the days of thy servant, and to add another year to my mortal life; I humbly beseech thee to take me under thy special care and protection for the time which is to come. As I grow in age, may I grow in grace, and so number my days that I may apply my heart unto wisdom. As I approach nearer and nearer the eternal world, may I live nearer and nearer to thee; and daily increase in thy Holy Spirit more and more, until I come unto thy everlasting kingdom; through Jesus Christ, my most blessed Saviour and Redeemer. *Amen.*

* To be used in private, or, with proper variations, in the family-prayer, for any member of the family.

Prayer after the Birth of a Child.

O ALMIGHTY GOD, we give thee humble thanks for thy gracious goodness to us as a family in preserving thy servant through the great pain and peril of childbirth; and may she show forth her own thankfulness in a renewed dedication of herself to thy service. And we beseech thee, O Lord, that the child now born unto us may be under thy special care and protection, and ever enjoy thy heavenly benediction. Mercifully support and preserve thy servant in her present need, and speedily restore her to her accustomed health and strength; and may this child be spared unto us in thy good Providence, and live to thy glory, to the comfort of its parents and friends, and, becoming a faithful member of thy holy Church, may finally be a partaker of thine everlasting kingdom; through Jesus Christ our Lord. *Amen.*

Before the Baptism of a Child.*

GRANT, O Lord, that the child who is this day to be dedicated to thee by the office and ministry which thou hast appointed, may receive thy blessing and heavenly benediction. Embrace *him*, O Lord, with the arms of thy mercy; give unto *him* the blessing of eternal life; and make *him* a partaker of thine everlasting kingdom. Thou hast said, "Suffer the little children to come unto me, and forbid them not"; and we would bring to thee this little one, not doubting that thou wilt favorably receive *him*, and beseeching thee that *he* may be sanctified by the Holy Ghost, and ever remain in the number of thy faithful children.

* To be used with the prayer for the morning.

After the Baptism of a Child.*

We humbly beseech thee O Father, that thy constant blessing may rest upon the child who has now been dedicated to thy service. May we faithfully discharge the solemn obligations which rest upon us, and train *him* up in thy faith and fear, teaching *him*, as soon as *he* is able to learn, what a solemn vow, promise, and profession have been made in *his* name, and calling upon *him* to remember thee, *his* Creator, in the days of *his* childhood and youth. And may we all, O Lord, be blessed of thee. May we be an united and happy family in thy love here on the earth, and finally be admitted to the Church triumphant in heaven, there to reign with thee world without end.

* To be used with the prayer for the evening.

After Confirmation.*

GRANT, O Lord, that thy blessing may rest upon all those who have this day, in their own persons, renewed the solemn vows and promises of their baptism, and received the laying on of hands. We especially commend to thee this thy servant who has participated in this holy rite. May *he* regard *himself* as solemnly consecrated to the service of Christ, and walking worthy of *his* high vocation, may *he* daily increase in thy Holy Spirit more and more, until *he* come unto thine everlasting kingdom.

For a Sick Member of the Family.

O FATHER of mercies, and God of all comfort, our only help in time of need; look

* To be used with the prayer for the evening.

FOR A SICK MEMBER OF THE FAMILY. 127

down from heaven, we humbly beseech thee, behold, visit, and relieve thy sick servant, for whom we offer up our earnest supplications. Look upon *him* with the eyes of thy mercy; comfort *him* with a sense of thy goodness; preserve *him* from the temptations of the enemy; give *him* patience under *his* afflic- tion; and, in thy good time, restore *him* to health, and enable *him* to lead the residue of *his* life in thy fear, and to thy glory: or else give *him* grace so to take thy visitation, that after this painful life ended, *he* may dwell with thee in life everlasting.

And we beseech thee, O Lord, to give us grace to submit to thy holy will in all thy dealings with us. Prepare us for all the events of thy providence. Make us deeply sensible of our exposure to sickness and to death, and may we always live in such a state that we may never be afraid nor unprepared to die. Regard us at this time with thy love and favor, and hear our prayers, through Jesus Christ. *Amen.*

Thanksgiving

FOR RECOVERY FROM SICKNESS.

WE bless thee, O God, for having turned our heaviness into joy, and our mourning into gladness, by delivering from *his* bodily sickness thy servant who is now enabled to unite with us in returning thanks unto thee for this thy great mercy. Gracious art thou, O Lord, and full of compassion to the children of men. May *his* heart be duly impressed with a sense of thy merciful goodness, and may *he* devote the residue of *his* days to an humble, holy, and obedient walking before thee.

And while we rejoice in this token of thy goodness towards us, we pray thee to make us deeply sensible of our sinfulness, and grant us grace to live more and more to the glory of thy Name, and to be ready at all times to yield up our spirits to thee, and to stand before thine awful bar. In all time of our tribulation, in all time of our prosperity, in the hour of death, and in the day of judgment, good Lord, deliver us, and save us, for Christ's sake. *Amen.*

A Sick Person's Prayer.

O LORD my God, it hath pleased thee to visit me with sickness, and thus to remind me of my dependence and frailty. Before I was afflicted I went astray, but now, O Lord, may I keep thy Word. Give me patience under this visitation of thy providence, and may I find thy grace to be sufficient for this time of need. May I be more desirous to have my sickness sanctified, than to have it removed. And yet, O Lord, may thy blessing attend the means that are used for my restoration to health; and wilt thou grant me a longer continuance here on the earth, that I may give all diligence to make my calling and election sure, and be prepared to meet thee in judgment.

O Lord, I would humble myself under thy hand, and truly repent of all my sins. O may they be washed away by the precious blood of Christ, and wilt thou visit me with thy salvation. And grant that I may be enabled to say, "It is good for me that I have been afflicted, that I might keep thy statutes"; so that whether I live, I may live unto thee, and whether I die, I may die unto thee; so that living and dying I may be thine, through Jesus Christ, my most blessed Redeemer. *Amen.*

For a Sick Child.

O ALMIGHTY GOD and merciful Father, to whom alone belong the issues of life and death; look down from heaven, we humbly beseech thee, with the eyes of mercy, upon this sick child. Visit *him*, O Lord, with thy salvation; deliver *him* in thy good appointed time from *his* bodily disease, and save his soul for thy mercies' sake; that if it shall be thy pleasure to prolong *his* days here on earth, *he* may live to thee, and be an instrument of thy glory, by serving thee faithfully, and doing good in *his* generation: or else, receive him into those heavenly habitations where the souls of those who sleep in the Lord Jesus enjoy perpetual rest and felicity.

Behold with pity, O Lord, our fears and sorrows. Restore, we beseech thee, this beloved child to our arms in health, and may *he* long live to our comfort and to thy glory, a member of Christ, a child of God, and an inheritor of the kingdom of heaven. Above all, we pray thee to make us submissive to thy will, and enable us at all times to say, "It is the Lord, let him do what seemeth to him good." Hear our prayer, O God, and let our cry come unto thee, through Jesus Christ our Saviour. *Amen.*

Thanksgiving

FOR THE RECOVERY OF A SICK CHILD.

ALMIGHTY FATHER, who, at the prayers of thy servants Elijah and Elisha didst gladden the hearts of two pious mothers by restoring them their dead; and who, by thy Son Jesus Christ, didst raise to health and life the children of many sorrowing parents; accept, we beseech thee, the thanks of thy *servants* who now praise thee for the deliverance of their dear child from sickness and the grave. May this recovered child be ever thine; and may our hearts so burn at the remembrance of thy goodness, that we may hold no thank-offering too costly to show forth thy praise, and may present ourselves, a living sacrifice, holy and acceptable unto thee, through the merits of Jesus Christ our Saviour. *Amen.*

Prayer

AFTER THE DEATH OF A MEMBER OF THE FAMILY.

O ETERNAL and merciful God, who hatest nothing that thou hast made, and hast compassion upon the children of men, we lift our eyes to thee as our only help in time of sorrow and affliction. In thy wisdom thou hast seen fit to visit us with trouble, and to bring distress upon us. Look upon us, O Lord, in mercy. Sanctify this thy fatherly correction to us; endue our souls with patience under this affliction, and with resignation to thy blessed will; comfort us with a sense of thy goodness; lift up thy countenance upon us, and give us peace.

O may we not mourn without hope, and may what seems so great a loss conduce to our eternal gain. With pious submission to thy unerring wisdom, may we resign the dear departed one to thy superior claim, and from our hearts be enabled to say, "The Lord gave, and the Lord hath taken away; blessed be the name of the Lord." May we feel that thou art just and good in all thy ways, and that thy mercy endureth for ever. May we neither despise thy chastening, nor faint under thy rebukes; but cheerfully submit to thy providential dealings, and put our whole trust and confidence in thy mercy.

And wilt thou make us deeply sensible, O Lord, of the shortness and uncertainty of human life; and when we shall have served thee in our generation, may we die the death of the righteous, and may our last end be like his.

Hear us, O merciful Father, in these our prayers, and dispose our ways towards the attainment of everlasting salvation, that among all the changes, trials, and sorrows of this mortal life, we may ever be defended by thy most gracious and ready help, through Jesus Christ our Lord. *Amen.*

Our Father, who art in Heaven, &c.

The grace of our Lord Jesus Christ, &c.

Prayer

FOR AN ABSENT MEMBER OF A FAMILY.*

O LORD our heavenly Father, whose mercy is over all thy works, we commend to thy protection and care thy servant now absent from *his* home and family. Be with *him* wherever he may be; guard *him* from every danger and calamity; keep *him* in health and safety; and return *him* to us in thy good providence, that we may praise thee for all thy mercies, through Jesus Christ our Saviour.

Prayer

FOR A CHILD ABSENT AT SCHOOL.†

MAY thy fatherly hand, O Lord, be over the absent member of our family, to shield *him* from every danger, and to guide *him* in

* To be used with the prayer for the morning or evening. With slight alteration, it may be used when a member of the family is about to leave home for a journey.

† To be used with the prayer for the morning or evening.

thy holy ways. May *he* faithfully improve the opportunities with which *he* is favored for gaining useful knowledge; and, above all things, may *he* gain that knowledge which maketh wise unto salvation. May *he* be submissive and obedient to those under whose charge *he* is placed; and may thy blessing rest upon their efforts to train up the young in the ways of wisdom and virtue. May *his* life and health be precious in thy sight; and may *he* finally obtain that life which is everlasting, through Jesus Christ our Saviour.

Thanksgiving for a Safe Return.*

MERCIFUL FATHER, we bless thee for thy good providence which has brought us together again in peace and safety, after our recent separation; and we pray thee to make us a happy family in thy love while on earth, and finally raise us to a heavenly home in thy kingdom, where there shall be no more parting, through Jesus Christ.

* To be used with the prayer for the morning or evening.

Prayer of Parents for their Children.

O THOU who art the merciful Parent of all the families of the earth, we, thine unworthy servants, come before thee to implore thy blessing upon the children that thou hast given us. O be thou their father and friend, and may they be thine own children, here and for ever. Guide them by thy providence through the dangers and temptations of a wicked world. Let thy fatherly hand, we beseech thee, ever be over them; let thy Holy Spirit ever be with them; and so lead them in the knowledge and obedience of thy word, that in the end they may obtain everlasting life.

And wilt thou, O Lord, give us wisdom and grace to bring them up in thy holy nurture and admonition. May we teach them all things which concern their eternal salvation, reminding them what a solemn vow, promise, and profession, were made for them at their baptism, instructing them in all the articles of the Christian faith, and giving all diligence to train them up in the way they should go, that when they are old they may not depart from it. May they early devote themselves to thy service, renewing the solemn promise and vow that have been made in their name, and daily increasing in thy Holy Spirit more and more, until they come unto thy everlasting kingdom. May they be dutiful and submissive, obeying their parents in the Lord, and honoring their father and mother, which is the first commandment with promise. May they love the Saviour who has declared his good will toward them, and be united to him by a living faith in his blessed Name. May the Holy Spirit dwell in their hearts as a Sanctifier and Guide; and, having been received into the ark of Christ's Church, being steadfast in faith, joyful through hope, and rooted in charity, may they so pass the waves of this troublesome world, that finally they may come to the land of everlasting life; through Jesus Christ our Lord. *Amen.*

Child's Morning Prayer.

ALMIGHTY and most merciful Father, I come to thee this morning to thank thee for thy goodness during the past night, and to ask thy blessing upon me this day. Direct me in all my ways, and be graciously pleased to take me, and all who are near and dear to me, under thy kind care and protection. Help me, O Lord, to give up all the sinful desires of my heart, to believe all the articles of the Christian faith, and obediently to keep thy holy will and commandments, and walk in the same all the days of my life. May I be dutiful and submissive to my dear parents, and gentle and kind to all, endeavoring to follow the example of the Holy Child Jesus, and to be made like unto him in all things. May I be truly a member of Christ, a child of God, and an inheritor of the kingdom of heaven. May I love thee more and more, and when all my days on earth have passed away, O receive me unto thyself in glory everlasting, for Christ's sake. *Amen.*

Our Father, who art in Heaven, Hallowed be thy Name. Thy Kingdom come. Thy Will be done on Earth, as it is in Heaven. Give us this day our daily bread. And forgive us our trespasses, as we forgive those who trespass against us. And lead us not into temptation; But deliver us from evil: For thine is the kingdom, and the power, and the glory, for ever and ever. Amen.

Child's Evening Prayer.

O Lord Jesus Christ, thou hast said, "Suffer little children to come unto me, and forbid them not"; and I come to ask thy blessing upon me this night. Thou hast suffered and died for my redemption, and I pray that I may cling to thy cross as all my hope.

May I love thee with all my heart, and keep all thy commandments. May thy grace be sufficient for me in every time of need. May I never be ashamed of thee and thy Gospel, and may I manfully fight under thy banner against sin, the world, and the devil, and continue thy faithful soldier and servant unto my life's end. Receive me, O Lord, into the arms of thy mercy; give unto me the blessing of eternal life; and make me a partaker of thine everlasting kingdom. Pardon, O Lord, the sins of this day, and make me, and all who are near and dear to me, obedient to thy will, that we may be happy here and for ever. *Amen.*

Our Father, who art in Heaven, &c.

Morning Prayer for a very Young Child.

O LORD, I thank thee for taking care of me all last night, when I was asleep. I thank thee that I am alive and well this morning. Keep me from all danger this day. May I not do anything that is wrong, but try to please thee, and my dear parents, by doing right; and may I at last go to heaven, and be happy for ever, for Jesus' sake. *Amen.*

Our Father, who art in Heaven, &c.

Evening Prayer for a very Young Child.

O LORD, I thank thee for thy care over me this day; and I pray thee to keep me safe this night. If I have done anything that is wrong, forgive me, for Jesus' sake, and may I do so no more. Bless my dear father and mother, [my dear brothers and sisters,] and all my friends, and make us all happy here and for ever. *Amen.*

Our Father, who art in Heaven, &c.

Now I lay me down to sleep,
I pray the Lord my soul to keep;
If I should die before I wake,
I pray the Lord my soul to take;
And this I ask for Jesus' sake.

Private Prayer.

MORNING.

O Lord my God, I am not worthy to come into thy presence, nor to call upon thy holy Name; but thou dost encourage thy dependent creatures to approach the throne of thy grace to ask those things which are requisite and necessary for them; and I therefore come, in Jesus' name, beseeching thee to hear the voice of my humble supplications.

O Lord, I acknowledge and bewail my manifold sins and wickedness, which, from time to time, I have most grievously committed, by thought, word, and deed, against thy Divine Majesty, provoking most justly thy wrath and indignation against me. O may I earnestly repent, and be heartily sorry for all my misdoings; may the remembrance of them be grievous unto me, and the burden of them intolerable. Have mercy upon me, have mercy upon me, most merciful Father; for thy Son our Lord Jesus Christ's sake, forgive me all that is past, and grant that I may ever hereafter serve and please thee in newness of life, to the honor and glory of thy Name.

Accept my thanks, O Lord, for thy merciful care over me the past night, and continue thy gracious protection to me this day. May I continually remember that thine eye is upon me, and that all my thoughts, and words, and actions, are known unto thee. Grant me thy Holy Spirit, to restrain me from sin, and to excite me to my duty. May I live this day as though I knew it was to be my last, having the solemn realities of eternity before my mind, and seeking those things which are above, where Christ sitteth at thy right hand.

May Christ, my blessed Redeemer, ever

dwell in my heart by faith; and, being rooted and grounded in love, may I be able to comprehend, with all saints, what is the breadth, and length, and depth, and height, and may I know the love of Christ, which passeth knowledge, and be filled with all the fulness of God. May the love of Christ constrain me, and may my life be hid with him in thee.

Preserve thou me, O Lord, from the sins which most easily beset me; cleanse me from my secret faults, and keep me from presumptuous sins, lest they get dominion over me. May I live near to thee, and may my fellowship be with thee and with thy Son Jesus Christ.

Hear me, O Lord my God, and bring me at last to those unspeakable joys which thou hast prepared for thy people, and which thou hast promised to those who unfeignedly love thee, through Jesus Christ my Strength and my Redeemer. *Amen.*

Our Father, who art in Heaven, &c.

Private Prayer.

EVENING.

O GOD, heavenly Father, I come before thee at the close of this day, to thank thee for thy kind care over me, and to ask that thy blessing may still rest upon me. I am weak and helpless, but thou art a strong tower to all those who put their trust in thee. Trusting in the multitude of thy tender mercies, and in thy loving-kindnesses which have been ever of old, I flee unto thee for rest and safety this night. Take me under the protection of thy good providence, and bring me to the beginning of another day.

O Lord, I humbly beseech thee to pardon whatever thou hast seen amiss in me this day. My misdeeds testify against me, and my trespasses are grown unto the heavens; but thy mercy also reacheth to the heavens, and thy truth unto the clouds. Be merciful, therefore, unto me, O God; be merciful unto me, for my soul trusteth in thee. Pardon and deliver me from all my sins; confirm and strengthen me in all goodness; and grant that I may henceforth obediently keep thy holy will and commandments.

May I remember that the time will soon come when I shall lie down in the dust, and sleep the sleep of death; and O may I have grace so to live that I may dread the grave as little as my bed, and never be unprepared to meet thee in judgment. May my whole trust and confidence be placed in thy mercy, through thy dear Son, and may I glory only in his atoning cross. May Christ be made unto me wisdom, and righteousness, and sanctification, and redemption. May I be united to him by a living faith, and follow his holy example. Preserve me from self-righteousness and self-reliance, and make me feel that Christ is all and in all. May thy Spirit bear witness with my spirit that I am among thine own children, and a joint-heir with Christ to the glories of thy heavenly kingdom.

And wilt thou, O Lord, make me diligent and active in all those good works which thou hast prepared for thy people to walk in. May I not be weary in well-doing; and, in the faithful use of all the means of grace which thou hast appointed, may I daily increase in thy Holy Spirit more and more, until I come unto thine everlasting kingdom. All which I humbly beg in the name and through the merits of Jesus Christ, my only Mediator and Advocate. *Amen.*

Our Father, who art in Heaven, &c.

To be included in the Private Prayer of a Husband or a Wife, with a proper variation of phraseology.

Bless, O Lord, my dear wife. May she have increasing evidence that she is a child of God, and enjoy that peace which the world cannot give. Help me to be to her a kind and faithful husband in all the changes and trials of life. Preserve me from fretfulness and impatience, and may we both be forbearing and forgiving. Bless her, O Lord, with all spiritual blessings in Christ Jesus.

Bless her with health and strength; and, if it be thy will, may we be spared to each other many years, and at last spend an eternity together in thy presence and joy. O may we both so grow in grace and holiness as to be for ever united in one and the same mansion in our Father's house on high. Bless, O Lord, our dear children, and help us to bring them up in thy holy nurture and admonition. May they be dutiful and obedient, and be made partakers of thy grace here, and of thy glory hereafter. Bless my dear parents, brothers, and sisters, and all my friends, and may we all, at last, meet around thy throne, to unite in the eternal praises of the redeemed, and to enjoy thy love and favor for ever and ever.

On Coming into Church.

O Lord, I am now in thy house; and may I remember that thine eye is upon me. Help me to worship thee with all my heart, and to hear thy Word with reverence and godly fear. Bless the whole congregation; may they worship thee in spirit and in truth, and receive with meekness the engrafted Word, which is able to save their souls. Bless him who ministers to us in thy Name; may the words of his mouth, and the meditation of his heart, be acceptable in thy sight, O Lord, my Strength and my Redeemer. *Amen.*

On Leaving Church.

O Lord, I thank thee for the privileges I have now enjoyed in thy house. I bless thee for the means of grace, and for the hope of glory. May I not forget what I have heard from thy holy Word; and may my worship be accepted, and my sins forgiven, for Jesus' sake. *Amen.*

Before or after Meals.

O Lord, bless to our use these gifts of thy providence; and give us grateful hearts for all thy mercies, for Christ's sake. *Amen.*

Grant thy blessing, O Lord, with these thy bounties; and nourish our souls with the bread of life, through Jesus Christ. *Amen.*

We thank thee, O Lord, for this and every expression of thy goodness; and may thy mercies lead us to thyself, through Jesus Christ. *Amen.*

Accept our thanks, O Lord, for these gifts of thy good providence; and as we live by thy mercy, may we live to thy glory, for Christ's sake. *Amen.*

The Collects

TO BE USED THROUGHOUT THE YEAR.

The first Sunday in Advent.

ALMIGHTY God, give us grace that we may cast away the works of darkness, and put upon us the armour of light, now in the time of this mortal life, in which thy Son Jesus Christ came to visit us in great humility; that in the last day, when he shall come again in his glorious Majesty to judge both the quick and the dead, we may rise to the life immortal, through him who liveth and reigneth with thee and the Holy Ghost, now and ever. *Amen.*

¶ *This Collect is to be repeated every day, with the other Collects in Advent, until Christmas Day.*

The second Sunday in Advent.

Blessed Lord, who hast caused all holy Scriptures to be written for our learning; Grant that we may in such wise hear them, read, mark, learn, and inwardly digest them, that by patience and comfort of thy holy Word, we may embrace, and ever hold fast the blessed hope of everlasting life, which thou hast given us in our Saviour Jesus Christ. *Amen.*

The third Sunday in Advent.

O Lord Jesus Christ, who at thy first coming didst send thy messenger to prepare thy way before thee; Grant that the ministers and stewards of thy mysteries may likewise so prepare and make ready thy way, by turning the hearts of the disobedient to the wisdom of the just, that at thy second coming to judge the world we may be found an acceptable people in thy sight, who livest and reignest with the Father and the Holy Spirit, ever one God, world without end. *Amen.*

The fourth Sunday in Advent.

O Lord, raise up, we pray thee, thy power, and come among us, and with great might succour us; that whereas, through our sins and wickedness, we are sore let and hindered in running the race that is set before us, thy bountiful grace and mercy may speedily help and deliver us ; through the satisfaction of thy Son our Lord, to whom, with thee and the Holy Ghost, be honour and glory, world without end. *Amen.*

The Nativity of our Lord, or the Birth-day of CHRIST, commonly called Christmas-day.

Almighty God, who hast given us thy only-begotten Son to take our nature upon him, and as at this time to be born of a pure Virgin ; Grant that we being regenerate, and made thy children by adoption and grace, may daily be renewed by thy Holy Spirit ; through the same our Lord Jesus Christ, who liveth and reigneth with thee and the same Spirit, ever one God, world without end. *Amen.*

Saint Stephen's Day.

Grant, O Lord, that, in all our sufferings here upon earth for the testimony of thy truth, we may steadfastly look up to heaven, and by faith behold the glory that shall be revealed ; and, being filled with the Holy Ghost, may learn to love and bless our persecutors by the example of thy first Martyr Saint Stephen, who prayed for his murderers to thee, O blessed Jesus, who standest at the right hand of God to succour all those that suffer for thee, our only Mediator and Advocate. *Amen.*

¶ *Then shall follow the Collect of the Nativity, which shall be said continually until New-Year's Eve.*

Saint John the Evangelist's Day.

Merciful Lord, we beseech thee to cast thy bright beams of light upon thy Church, that it being instructed by the doctrine of thy blessed Apostle and Evangelist Saint John, may so walk in the light of thy truth, that it may at length attain to everlasting life; through Jesus Christ our Lord. *Amen.*

The Innocents' Day.

O Almighty God, who out of the mouths of babes and sucklings hast ordained strength, and madest infants to glorify thee by their deaths; Mortify and kill all vices in us, and so strengthen us by thy grace, that by the innocency of our lives, and constancy of our faith, even unto death, we may glorify thy holy Name; through Jesus Christ our Lord. *Amen.*

The Sunday after Christmas Day.

Almighty God, who hast given us thy only-begotten Son to take our nature upon him, and as at this time to be born of a pure Virgin; Grant that we being regenerate, and made thy children by adoption and grace, may daily be renewed by thy Holy Spirit; through the same our Lord Jesus Christ, who liveth and reigneth with thee and the same Spirit, ever one God, world without end. *Amen.*

The Circumcision of Christ.

Almighty God, who madest thy blessed Son to be circumcised, and obedient to the law for man; Grant us the true Circumcision of the Spirit; that, our hearts, and all our members, being mortified from all worldly and carnal lusts, we may in all things obey thy blessed will; through the same thy Son Jesus Christ our Lord. *Amen.*

¶ *The same Collect shall serve for every day after unto the Epiphany.*

The Epiphany, or the Manifestation of Christ to the Gentiles.

O God, who by the leading of a star didst manifest thy only-begotten Son to the Gentiles; Mercifully grant, that we, who know thee now by faith, may after this life have the fruition of thy glorious Godhead; through Jesus Christ our Lord. *Amen.*

The first Sunday after the Epiphany.

O Lord, we beseech thee mercifully to receive the prayers of thy people who call upon thee; and grant that they may both perceive and know what things they ought to do, and also may have grace and power faithfully to fulfil the same; through Jesus Christ our Lord. *Amen.*

The second Sunday after the Epiphany.

Almighty and everlasting God, who dost govern all things in heaven and earth; Mercifully hear the supplications of thy people, and grant us thy peace all the days of our life; through Jesus Christ our Lord. *Amen.*

The third Sunday after the Epiphany.

Almighty and everlasting God, mercifully look upon our infirmities, and in all dangers and necessities stretch forth thy right hand to help and defend us; through Jesus Christ our Lord. *Amen.*

The fourth Sunday after the Epiphany.

O God, who knowest us to be set in the midst of so many and great dangers, that by reason of the frailty of our nature we cannot always stand upright; Grant to us such strength and protection, as may support us in all dangers, and carry us through all temptations; through Jesus Christ our Lord. Amen.

The fifth Sunday after the Epiphany.

O Lord, we beseech thee to keep thy Church and household continually in thy true religion; that they who do lean only upon the hope of thy heavenly grace may evermore be defended by thy mighty power; through Jesus Christ our Lord. Amen.

The sixth Sunday after the Epiphany.

O God, whose blessed Son was manifested that he might destroy the works of the devil, and make us the sons of God, and heirs of eternal life; Grant us, we beseech thee, that, having this hope, we may purify ourselves, even as he is pure; that, when he shall appear again with power and great glory, we may be made like unto him in his eternal and glorious kingdom ; wherewith thee, O Father, and thee, O Holy Ghost, he liveth and reigneth, ever one God, world without end. *Amen.*

The Sunday called Septuagesima, or the third Sunday before Lent.

O Lord, we beseech thee favourably to hear the prayers of thy people ; that we who are justly punished for our offences, may be mercifully delivered by thy goodness, for the glory of thy Name ; through Jesus Christ our Saviour, who liveth and reigneth with thee and the Holy Ghost, ever one God, world without end. *Amen.*

The Sunday called Sexagesima, or the second Sunday before Lent.

O Lord God, who seest that we put not our trust in any thing that we do ; Mercifully grant that by thy power we may be defended against all adversity ; through Jesus Christ our Lord. *Amen.*

The Sunday called Quinquagesima, or the next Sunday before Lent.

O Lord, who hast taught us that all our

doings without charity are nothing worth; Send thy Holy Ghost, and pour into our hearts that most excellent gift of charity, the very bond of peace and of all virtues, without which whosoever liveth is counted dead before thee: Grant this for thine only Son Jesus Christ's sake. *Amen.*

The first day of Lent, commonly called Ash-Wednesday.

Almighty and everlasting God, who hatest nothing that thou hast made, and dost forgive the sins of all those who are penitent; Create and make in us new and contrite hearts, that we worthily lamenting our sins, and acknowledging our wretchedness, may obtain of thee, the God of all mercy, perfect remission and forgiveness; through Jesus Christ our Lord. *Amen.*

¶ *This Collect is to be read every day in Lent, after the Collect appointed for the Day.*

The first Sunday in Lent.

O Lord, who for our sake didst fast forty days and forty nights; Give us grace to use such abstinence, that, our flesh being subdued to the Spirit, we may ever obey thy godly motions in righteousness, and true holiness, to thy honour and glory, who livest and reignest with the Father and the Holy Ghost, one God, world without end. *Amen.*

The second Sunday in Lent.

Almighty God, who seest that we have no power of ourselves to help ourselves; Keep us both outwardly in our bodies, and inwardly in our souls; that we may be defended from all adversities which may happen to the body, and from all evil thoughts which may assault and hurt the soul; through Jesus Christ our Lord. *Amen.*

The third Sunday in Lent.

We beseech thee, Almighty God, look upon the hearty desires of thy humble servants, and stretch forth the right hand of thy Majesty, to be our defence against all our enemies; through Jesus Christ our Lord. *Amen.*

The fourth Sunday in Lent.

Grant, we beseech thee, Almighty God, that we, who for our evil deeds do worthily deserve to be punished, by the comfort of thy grace may mercifully be relieved; through our Lord and Saviour Jesus Christ. *Amen.*

The fifth Sunday in Lent.

We beseech thee, Almighty God, mercifully to look upon thy people; that by thy great goodness they may be governed and preserved evermore, both in body and soul; through Jesus Christ our Lord. *Amen.*

The Sunday next before Easter.

Almighty and everlasting God, who, of thy tender love towards mankind, hast sent thy Son our Saviour Jesus Christ, to take upon him our flesh, and to suffer death upon the cross, that all mankind should follow the example of his great humility; Mercifully grant, that we may both follow the example of his patience, and also be made partakers of his resurrection; through the same Jesus Christ our Lord. *Amen.*

GOOD FRIDAY.

Almighty God, we beseech thee graciously to behold this thy family, for which our Lord Jesus Christ was contented to be betrayed, and given up into the hands of wicked men, and to suffer death upon the cross, who now liveth and reigneth with thee and the Holy Ghost, ever one God, world without end. *Amen.*

Almighty and everlasting God, by whose Spirit the whole body of the Church is governed and sanctified; Receive our supplications and prayers, which we offer before thee for all estates of men in thy holy Church, that every member of the same, in his vocation and ministry, may truly and godly serve thee; through our Lord and Saviour Jesus Christ. *Amen.*

O merciful God, who hast made all men, and hatest nothing that thou hast made, nor desirest the death of a sinner, but rather that he should be converted and live; Have mercy upon all Jews, Turks, Infidels, and Heretics; and take from them all ignorance, hardness of heart, and contempt of thy Word; and so fetch them home, blessed Lord, to thy flock, that they may be saved among the remnant of the true Israelites, and be made one fold under one Shepherd, Jesus Christ our Lord, who liveth and reigneth with thee and the Holy Spirit, one God, world without end. *Amen.*

Easter Even.

Grant, O Lord, that as we are baptized into the death of thy blessed Son our Saviour Jesus Christ, so by continual mortifying our corrupt affections we may be buried with him; and that through the grave, and gate of death, we may pass to our joyful resurrection; for his merits, who died, and was buried, and rose again for us, thy Son Jesus Christ our Lord. *Amen.*

EASTER DAY.

Almighty God, who through thine only-begotten Son Jesus Christ hast overcome death, and opened unto us the gate of everlasting life; We humbly beseech thee, that, as by thy special grace preventing us thou dost put into our minds good desires, so by thy continual help we may bring the same to good effect; through Jesus Christ our Lord, who liveth and reigneth with thee and the Holy Ghost, ever one God, world without end. *Amen.*

¶ *This Collect serves for Monday and Tuesday in Easter-week.*

The first Sunday after Easter.

Almighty Father, who hast given thine only

Son to die for our sins, and to rise again for our justification; Grant us so to put away the leaven of malice and wickedness, that we may always serve thee in pureness of living and truth; through the merits of the same thy Son Jesus Christ our Lord. *Amen.*

The second Sunday after Easter.

Almighty God, who hast given thine only Son to be unto us both a sacrifice for sin, and also an ensample of godly life; Give us grace that we may always most thankfully receive that his inestimable benefit, and also daily endeavour ourselves to follow the blessed steps of his most holy life; through the same Jesus Christ our Lord. *Amen.*

The third Sunday after Easter.

Almighty God, who showest to them that are in error the light of thy truth, to the intent that they may return into the way of righteousness; Grant unto all those who are admitted into the fellowship of Christ's Religion, that they may avoid those things that are contrary to their profession, and follow all such things as are agreeable to the same; through our Lord Jesus Christ. *Amen*

The fourth Sunday after Easter.

O Almighty God, who alone canst order the unruly wills and affections of sinful men; Grant unto thy people, that they may love the thing which thou commandest, and desire that which thou dost promise; that so, among the sundry and manifold changes of the world, our hearts may surely there be fixed, where true joys are to be found; through Jesus Christ our Lord. *Amen.*

The fifth Sunday after Easter.

O Lord, from whom all good things do come; Grant to us thy humble servants, that by thy holy inspiration we may think those things that are good, and by thy merciful guiding may perform the same; through our Lord Jesus Christ. *Amen.*

Ascension Day.

Grant, we beseech thee, Almighty God, that like as we do believe thy only-begotten Son our Lord Jesus Christ to have ascended into the heavens; so we may also in heart and mind thither ascend, and with him continually dwell, who liveth and reigneth with thee and the Holy Ghost, one God, world without end. *Amen.*

Sunday after Ascension Day.

O God, the King of glory, who hast exalted thine only Son Jesus Christ with great triumph unto thy kingdom in heaven ; We beseech thee, leave us not comfortless ; but send to us thine Holy Ghost to comfort us, and exalt us unto the same place whither our Saviour Christ is gone before, who liveth and reigneth with thee and the Holy Ghost, one God, world without end. *Amen.*

WHIT-SUNDAY.

O God, who as at this time didst teach the hearts of thy faithful people, by sending to them the light of thy Holy Spirit ; Grant us by the same Spirit to have a right judgment in all things, and evermore to rejoice in his holy comfort ; through the merits of Christ Jesus our Saviour, who liveth and reigneth with thee, in the unity of the same Spirit, one God, world without end. *Amen.*

¶ *This Collect serves for Monday and Tuesday in Whitsun-week.*

TRINITY-SUNDAY.

Almighty and everlasting God, who hast given unto us thy servants grace, by the confession of a true faith, to acknowledge the glory of the eternal Trinity, and in the power of the Divine Majesty to worship the Unity; We beseech thee, that thou wouldest keep us steadfast in this faith, and evermore defend us from all adversities, who livest and reignest, one God, world without end. *Amen.*

The first Sunday after Trinity.

O God, the strength of all those who put their trust in thee; Mercifully accept our prayers, and because through the weakness of our mortal nature, we can do no good thing without thee, grant us the help of thy grace, that in keeping thy commandments we may please thee, both in will and deed; through Jesus Christ our Lord. *Amen.*

The second Sunday after Trinity.

O Lord, who never failest to help and govern those whom thou dost bring up in thy steadfast fear and love; Keep us, we beseech thee, under the protection of thy good providence, and make us to have a perpetual fear and love of thy holy Name; through Jesus Christ our Lord. *Amen.*

The third Sunday after Trinity.

O Lord, we beseech thee mercifully to hear us; and grant that we, to whom thou hast given an hearty desire to pray, may, by thy mighty aid, be defended and comforted in all dangers and adversities; through Jesus Christ our Lord. *Amen.*

The fourth Sunday after Trinity.

O God, the protector of all that trust in thee, without whom nothing is strong, nothing is holy; Increase and multiply upon us thy mercy; that, thou being our ruler and guide, we may so pass through things temporal, that we finally lose not the things eternal. Grant this, O heavenly Father, for Jesus Christ's sake our Lord. *Amen.*

The fifth Sunday after Trinity.

Grant, O Lord, we beseech thee, that the course of this world may be so peaceably ordered by thy governance, that thy Church may joyfully serve thee in all godly quietness; through Jesus Christ our Lord. *Amen.*

The sixth Sunday after Trinity.

O God, who hast prepared for those who love thee such good things as pass man's understanding; Pour into our hearts such love toward thee, that we, loving thee above all things, may obtain thy promises, which exceed all that we can desire; through Jesus Christ our Lord. *Amen.*

The seventh Sunday after Trinity

Lord of all power and might, who art the author and giver of all good things; Graft in our hearts the love of thy Name, increase in us true religion, nourish us with all goodness, and of thy great mercy keep us in the same; through Jesus Christ our Lord. *Amen.*

The eighth Sunday after Trinity.

O God, whose never-failing providence ordereth all things both in heaven and earth; We humbly beseech thee to put away from us all hurtful things, and to give us those things which are profitable for us; through Jesus Christ our Lord. *Amen.*

THE COLLECTS. 171

The ninth Sunday after Trinity.

Grant to us, Lord, we beseech thee, the spirit to think and do always such things as are right; that we, who cannot do any thing that is good without thee, may by thee be enabled to live according to thy will, through Jesus Christ our Lord. *Amen.*

The tenth Sunday after Trinity.

Let thy merciful ears, O Lord, be open to the prayers of thy humble servants; and that they may obtain their petitions make them to ask such things as shall please thee; through Jesus Christ our Lord. *Amen.*

The eleventh Sunday after Trinity.

O God, who declarest thy almighty power chiefly in showing mercy and pity; Mercifully grant unto us such a measure of thy grace, that we, running the way of thy commandments, may obtain thy gracious promises, and be made partakers of thy heavenly treasure; through Jesus Christ our Lord. *Amen.*

The twelfth Sunday after Trinity.

Almighty and everlasting God, who art always more ready to hear than we to pray, and art wont to give more than either we desire or deserve; Pour down upon us the abundance of thy mercy; forgiving us those things whereof our conscience is afraid, and giving us those good things which we are not worthy to ask, but through the merits and mediation of Jesus Christ, thy Son, our Lord. *Amen.*

The thirteenth Sunday after Trinity.

Almighty and merciful God, of whose only gift it cometh that thy faithful people do unto thee true and laudable service; Grant, we beseech thee, that we may so faithfully serve thee in this life, that we fail not finally to attain thy heavenly promises; through the merits of Jesus Christ our Lord. *Amen.*

The fourteenth Sunday after Trinity.

Almighty and everlasting God, give unto us the increase of faith, hope, and charity; and, that we may obtain that which thou dost promise, make us to love that which thou dost command; through Jesus Christ our Lord. *Amen.*

The fifteenth Sunday after Trinity.

Keep, we beseech thee, O Lord, thy Church

with thy perpetual mercy; and, because the frailty of man without thee cannot but fall, keep us ever by thy help from all things hurtful, and lead us to all things profitable to our salvation; through Jesus Christ our Lord. *Amen.*

The sixteenth Sunday after Trinity.

O Lord, we beseech thee, let thy continual pity cleanse and defend thy Church; and, because it cannot continue in safety without thy succour, preserve it evermore by thy help and goodness; through Jesus Christ our Lord. *Amen.*

The seventeenth Sunday after Trinity.

Lord, we pray thee that thy grace may always prevent and follow us, and make us continually to be given to all good works; through Jesus Christ our Lord. *Amen.*

The eighteenth Sunday after Trinity.

Lord, we beseech thee, grant thy people grace to withstand the temptations of the world, the flesh, and the devil, and with pure hearts and minds to follow thee the only God; through Jesus Christ our Lord. *Amen.*

The nineteenth Sunday after Trinity.

O God, forasmuch as without thee we are not able to please thee; Mercifully grant that thy Holy Spirit may in all things direct and rule our hearts; through Jesus Christ our Lord. Amen.

The twentieth Sunday after Trinity.

O Almighty and most merciful God, of thy bountiful goodness keep us, we beseech thee, from all things that may hurt us; that we, being ready both in body and soul, may cheerfully accomplish those things which thou commandest; through Jesus Christ our Lord. Amen.

The twenty-first Sunday after Trinity.

Grant, we beseech thee, merciful Lord, to thy faithful people pardon and peace; that they may be cleansed from all their sins, and serve thee with a quiet mind; through Jesus Christ our Lord. Amen.

The twenty-second Sunday after Trinity.

Lord, we beseech thee to keep thy household the Church in continual godliness; that

THE COLLECTS. 175

through thy protection it may be free from all adversities, and devoutly given to serve thee in good works, to the glory of thy Name; through Jesus Christ our Lord. *Amen.*

The twenty-third Sunday after Trinity.

O God, our refuge and strength, who art the author of all godliness; Be ready, we beseech thee, to hear the devout prayers of thy Church; and grant that those things which we ask faithfully we may obtain effectually; through Jesus Christ our Lord. *Amen.*

The twenty-fourth Sunday after Trinity.

O Lord, we beseech thee, absolve thy people from their offences; that through thy bountiful goodness we may all be delivered from the bands of those sins, which by our frailty we have committed. Grant this, O heavenly Father, for Jesus Christ's sake, our blessed Lord and Saviour. *Amen.*

The twenty-fifth Sunday after Trinity

Stir up, we beseech thee, O Lord, the wills of thy faithful people; that they, plenteously bringing forth the fruit of good works, may by thee be plenteously rewarded; through Jesus Christ our Lord. *Amen.*

¶ *If there be any more Sundays before Advent-Sunday, the Collects of some of those Sundays that were omitted after the Epiphany shall be taken in to supply so many as are here wanting. And if there be fewer, the overplus may be omitted: Provided that this last Collect shall always be used upon the Sunday next before Advent.*

St. Andrew's Day.

Almighty God, who didst give such grace unto thy holy Apostle Saint Andrew, that he readily obeyed the calling of thy Son Jesus Christ, and followed him without delay; Grant unto us all, that we, being called by thy holy Word, may forthwith give up ourselves obediently to fulfil thy holy commandments; through the same Jesus Christ our Lord. *Amen.*

Saint Thomas the Apostle.

Almighty and everliving God, who, for the greater confirmation of the faith, didst suffer thy holy Apostle Thomas to be doubtful in thy Son's resurrection; Grant us so perfectly, and without all doubt, to believe in thy Son Jesus Christ, that our faith in thy sight may never be reproved. Hear us, O Lord, through the same Jesus Christ, to whom, with thee and the Holy

Ghost, be all honour and glory, now and for evermore. *Amen.*

The Conversion of Saint Paul.

O God, who, through the preaching of the blessed Apostle Saint Paul, hast caused the light of the Gospel to shine throughout the world; Grant, we beseech thee, that we, having his wonderful conversion in remembrance, may show forth our thankfulness unto thee for the same, by following the holy doctrine which he taught; through Jesus Christ our Lord. *Amen.*

The Presentation of Christ in the Temple, commonly called, The Purification of Saint Mary the Virgin.

Almighty and everliving God, we humbly beseech thy Majesty, that, as thy only-begotten Son was this day presented in the temple in substance of our flesh, so we may be presented unto thee with pure and clean hearts, by the same thy Son Jesus Christ our Lord. *Amen.*

Saint Matthias's Day.

O Almighty God, who into the place of the

traitor Judas didst choose thy faithful servant Matthias to be of the number of the twelve Apostles; Grant that thy Church, being always preserved from false Apostles, may be ordered and guided by faithful and true pastors; through Jesus Christ our Lord. *Amen.*

The Annunciation of the Blessed Virgin Mary.

We beseech thee, O Lord, pour thy grace into our hearts; that, as we have known the incarnation of thy Son Jesus Christ by the message of an Angel, so by his cross and passion we may be brought unto the glory of his resurrection; through the same Jesus Christ our Lord. *Amen.*

Saint Mark's Day.

O Almighty God, who hast instructed thy holy Church with the heavenly doctrine of thy Evangelist Saint Mark; Give us grace that, being not like children carried away with every blast of vain doctrine, we may be established in the truth of thy holy Gospel; through Jesus Christ our Lord. *Amen.*

Saint Philip and Saint James's Day.

O Almighty God, whom truly to know is

everlasting life; Grant us perfectly to know thy Son Jesus Christ to be the way, the truth, and the life; that, following the steps of thy holy Apostles, Saint Philip and Saint James, we may steadfastly walk in the way that leadeth to eternal life; through the same thy Son Jesus Christ our Lord. *Amen.*

Saint Barnabas the Apostle.

O Lord God Almighty, who didst endue thy holy Apostle Barnabas with singular gifts of the Holy Ghost; Leave us not, we beseech thee, destitute of thy manifold gifts, nor yet of grace to use them alway to thy honour and glory; through Jesus Christ our Lord. *Amen.*

Saint John Baptist's Day.

Almighty God, by whose providence thy servant John Baptist was wonderfully born, and sent to prepare the way of thy Son our Saviour, by preaching repentance; Make us so to follow his doctrine and holy life, that we may truly repent according to his preaching; and after his example constantly speak the truth, boldly rebuke vice, and patiently suffer for the truth's sake; through Jesus Christ our Lord. *Amen.*

Saint Peter's Day.

O Almighty God, who by thy Son Jesus Christ didst give to thy Apostle Saint Peter many excellent gifts, and commandedst him earnestly to feed thy flock; Make, we beseech thee, all Bishops and Pastors diligently to preach thy holy Word, and the people obediently to follow the same, that they may receive the crown of everlasting glory; through Jesus Christ our Lord. *Amen.*

Saint James the Apostle.

Grant, O merciful God, that as thine holy Apostle Saint James, leaving his father and all that he had, without delay was obedient unto the calling of thy Son Jesus Christ, and followed him; so we, forsaking all worldly and carnal affections, may be evermore ready to follow thy holy commandments; through Jesus Christ our Lord. *Amen.*

Saint Bartholomew the Apostle.

O Almighty and everlasting God, who didst give thine Apostle Bartholomew grace truly to believe and to preach thy Word; Grant, we beseech thee, unto thy Church, to love that Word which he believed, and both to preach and receive the same ; through Jesus Christ our Lord. *Amen.*

Saint Matthew the Apostle.

O Almighty God, who by thy blessed Son didst call Matthew from the receipt of custom to be an Apostle and Evangelist; Grant us grace to forsake all covetous desires, and inordinate love of riches, and to follow the same thy Son Jesus Christ, who liveth and reigneth with thee and the Holy Ghost, one God, world without end. *Amen*

Saint Michael and all Angels.

O Everlasting God, who hast ordained and constituted the services of Angels and men in a wonderful order; Mercifully grant, that as thy holy Angels always do thee service in heaven, so, by thy appointment, they may succour and defend us on earth; through Jesus Christ our Lord. *Amen.*

Saint Luke the Evangelist.

Almighty God, who calledst Luke the Physician, whose praise is in the Gospel, to be an

Evangelist, and Physician of the soul; May it please thee, that, by the wholesome medicines of the doctrine delivered by him, all the diseases of our souls may be healed; through the merits of thy Son Jesus Christ our Lord. *Amen.*

Saint Simon and Saint Jude, Apostles.

O Almighty God, who hast built thy Church upon the foundation of the Apostles and Prophets, Jesus Christ himself being the head corner-stone; Grant us so to be joined together in unity of spirit by their doctrine, that we may be made an holy temple acceptable unto thee; through Jesus Christ our Lord. *Amen.*

All Saints' Day.

O Almighty God, who hast knit together thine elect in one communion and fellowship, in the mystical body of thy Son Christ our Lord; Grant us grace so to follow thy blessed Saints in all virtuous and godly living, that we may come to those unspeakable joys, which thou hast prepared for those who unfeignedly love thee; through Jesus Christ our Lord. *Amen.*